Ea
Thoughts
Western Mind

Insights on
Raja Yoga Meditation

Anthony Strano

Eastern Thought for the Western Mind
Insights on Raja Yoga Meditation

Anthony Strano

First Edition 2006

ISBN: 1-886872-28-7

Published by Brahma Kumaris Information Services Ltd., in
association with Brahma Kumaris World Spiritual University
(UK) Registered Charity No. 269971.
Global Co-operation House, 65 Pound Lane,
London NW10 2HH, UK

Designed by BookDesign™, London
Printed by Power Digital Printing Co Ltd. Hong Kong

www.bkpublications.com
email: enquiries@bkpublications.com

www.bkwsu.org

Eastern Thought for the Western Mind

Insights on
Raja Yoga Meditation

Anthony Strano

BK PUBLICATIONS
an imprint of
BRAHMA KUMARIS INFORMATION SERVICES LTD.

ABOUT THE AUTHOR

ANTHONY STRANO has been practising and teaching Raja
Yoga meditation with the Brahma Kumaris World Spiritual
University for nearly 30 years. Born in Australia, he has lived
in Italy, Hungary, Turkey and Greece where he is currently
based in Athens. He travels internationally giving lectures,
conducting workshops and seminars on the practical
application of spiritual ideas. He is the author of three
previous publications: *The Alpha Point - a glimpse of God;
Discovering Spirituality* and *Reflections*

PREFACE

RAJA YOGA MEDITATION gently and naturally opens the doors of our perception, producing insights and experiences that bring lasting change in our lives. It heals old wounds and restores our capacity to love, to learn and adapt, and to envision and build a better future.

Anthony Strano has been dedicatedly prising open these doors for the past 30 years and in this book he shares some of the rich treasures of spiritual understanding and strength that he has acquired. As one of the first students of Raja Yoga from outside India in modern times, he has developed an exceptional ability to communicate the essence of his findings to a Western audience.

As well as sharing these insights in a fresh and stimulating way, his book offers practical guidance on how to enable the light that enters a silent mind to awaken and refine our understanding and experience. The result of such awakening is that our interactions with others become based on respect and love, instead of selfishness and dependence – a transformation that the whole world awaits and needs.

CONTENTS

1

EASTERN THOUGHT FOR THE WESTERN MIND

NOWADAYS, THE MAJORITY of people in the West who wish to learn how to meditate do so because they want to relax. In a world of constant demands, where everything appears to happen at lightning speed, people want to learn the technique of freeing themselves from the variety of tensions they face, find an inner calm to bring about balance in their lives and sustain a positive frame of mind.

In the East, meditation is an ancient tradition, which involves far more than just relaxing and being positive; it is a way to enlighten the mind. An enlightened mind is one filled with peace, clarity and kindness. Clarity enables the individual to make decisions, which are benevolent and accurate for the self and others; kindness protects the self and others from the harmful effects of the mind's negative desires. The aim of meditation is to use the values of wisdom, peace and kindness to enable the individual to control the mind, to keep it in order.

However, even in ancient times, the mind was understood to be extremely difficult to control. It was said to be like the wind: you could never catch it, or hold it – it went where it wished and no human being could become its master. In other instances, it was said that the mind was like an elephant: extremely powerful but equally gentle and patient, able to do a lot of work for its master. However, when an elephant turns wild, its gentleness and patience completely disappear and it destroys and damages everything in its path. When the mind is under stress, it resembles a wild elephant, it has no control and cannot be controlled.

Taming the mind is regarded as a great art requiring time, attention, practice and, above all, a sincerity of heart where individuals truly want to change their way of thinking. To relax, to be positive, to be peaceful and kind all require a change in our thought patterns and this can only happen when we look deeply within. However hard they try, other people cannot change us; we must have personal realisation and the desire to make changes through our own effort. Permanent and positive change cannot be imposed from outside; it is something that we choose.

Meditation is the discovery of that point of silence within, like a compass needle that guides us in the right direction at the right time. To become silent, to be still in the ocean of hectic, noisy action, is a choice many people are now making. When this is achieved, this stillness acts on the mind like oxygen, giving the breath to both understand and enrich life. Of course, action is a necessity, an expression of ourselves through time, relationships and the roles we play. However, if we do not sometimes stop and take a breath of silence, then the mind begins to suffocate, thoughts speed like bullet trains and the brain feels as if it is in a pressure cooker. Emotions erupt and react like volcanoes, the eyes become dizzy with mountains of information and the head feels like a rollercoaster. This is stress. The mind needs to come up for air, to leave the jungle of pressures, deadlines and speed and slow down and find the point of silence within.

Meditation is the method to find that point which recharges the mind with peace, clarity and balance.

We can define meditation as the eight 'Rs':

1. Returning

Meditation is the technique of returning to the original qualities of the self, namely peace, purity, love, bliss and wisdom. We can only do that by taking our thoughts inwards.

> *I begin to find my original strength by collecting the energy of my mind. With my concentrated thought, I focus on meeting my real self.*

2. Relaxing

In meditation, the mind disconnects itself from the thoughts of anything external and connects with the inner self. In this way, it is able to receive the positive current of the original strength of the self: a peaceful source of energy. However, at first, it can be difficult to disconnect the many plugs of our everyday life: the plugs of attachment, speed, worry, being busy, etc. It does take some effort.

> *As I connect to the 'point source' of energy of the self, which is located in the centre of the forehead, I start to relax, to remove the many tensions and demands of the outside world from the mind.*

3. Remembering

As the mind relaxes and gently concentrates on the 'point source' of peace energy, the individual begins to remember their spiritual identity. The reason why people are so disorientated in their lives and why they often find life boring, tedious, or empty is because they have forgotten who they truly are.

> *In silence, going inwards, I begin to remember what I have forgotten: I am a spiritual being, a point source of positive energy. My spirit is my reality!*

4. Releasing

As we remember the forgotten reality of the self as a spiritual being and begin to experience our inner source of peace, we are released from the negativity of our mind: wasteful thinking and thoughts filled with doubt, fear and worry - the three great dragons that dominate our mind constantly.

> *As I begin to rule my own mind, I free myself from the worry that cripples my confidence, from the fear that hijacks my courage and the doubt, which ridicules every attempt I make to bring hope back into my life.*

5. Relearning

As we become free, we begin to respect ourselves and relearn what it means to value our self, our life and our existence in this great play of life. Forgotten truths appear and a new education of the self begins.

> *I am able to understand eternity and spirituality and feelings of my true humanity emerge.*

6. Rediscovering

As we relearn, we rediscover our spiritual values and resources and, realising they were always there, we resolve to use these silent intrinsic truths, which are the foundation of a better quality of life.

> *I am a positive, purposeful being, who has something unique to offer to life.*

7. Restoring

As we begin to use these spiritual truths, our original strengths and qualities are restored. There is a transition in consciousness enabling confidence and self-esteem to become a natural way of being.

I value myself as a being of peace and love and know that I have within me all the qualities I need to overcome all the challenges of life.

8. Recharging

The leap of consciousness that occurs when we connect with our inner spiritual self, is a powerful way of recharging the energies of the human mind. It is filled with a deep tranquillity that flows into our thoughts and is then reflected in our words and actions. A world of new vision opens where there is self-mastery and acceptance of life as it is.

I have the inner strength to let go of judgements, dissatisfaction, impatience and replace negative energies with a more positive outlook.

2

QUALITY CHANGE

QUALITY CHANGE IS the capacity to transform 'negative' situations, or circumstances, into something beneficial for one's self and others. 'Quality transformers' are people who can turn walls of resistance into bridges of understanding and keep crossing them, who can change any obstacle into a stepping stone of success and can reverse the niggling, paralysing dragon of doubt into radiant self-confidence, dissolving the thought 'impossible' from the mind.

Such people work with the undercurrents of life that determine the external reality of human interaction, namely their attitudes, thoughts and feelings. If these are permeated with resentment, anger and selfishness, then, despite a façade of politeness or cooperation, relationships will be subject to damage and deterioration. On the other hand, when the undercurrent is one of trust and sincerity, then the quality of life is enhanced. The fundamental source of quality is the existence of a positive undercurrent. It is not a matter of words, actions or role, but rather the foundation of these, manifested in thoughts and the activity of the mind.

Meditation enables the mind to tune in to that undercurrent of thoughts, feelings, and attitudes, which is the invisible creator of our human reality. The nourishing power of silence, attained through meditation and spiritual knowledge, gives us the means to create quality change. Such change enhances our self-confidence and the capacity to creatively and positively relate to life as it is.

Silence gives us the energy necessary to effect change and self knowledge gives us the perception and insight to realise the opportunity for change that everyone and every situation offers.

How do we qualitatively transform ourselves? Is it something we plan and consciously do? Does it just happen by itself? Or, is it a state of awareness that naturally recognises opportunities for quality change?

The easiest way to understand quality change came to me one day when I had to put fresh smelly, manure around the roses in my garden. After a few hours of this work, I realised that those beautiful flowers, although nourished by the manure, did not take any of its odour or colour. They were truly like kings of the garden, in their pink, gold, red and white robes, filling the air with such a fragrance that people who came to the garden did not even notice the manure. The roots of the roses were able to transform the manure to such an extent that the best was taken without any negative side effects. This was my first experience of quality change.

The human world is like a garden. We are like a variety of flowers surrounded by lots of manure, that is, negativity in all its forms, such as ego, fear, anger, attachment, mistrust, etc. People who are 'quality transformers' can accept all these negative things and use them for their personal growth without the negativity penetrating them; they do not get spoilt, or even touched by it. With understanding and the natural, loving detachment that comes from silence, they realise that the negative person, or situation, in front of them is the Universe's way of giving them an opportunity to create a tiny, silent miracle in their lives. Quality transformers become the spiritual roses in the Garden of Humanity: they display all their beauty and provide inspiration for all those who see them.

'Quality transformers' can also be compared to the oyster - when a tiny foreign particle invades its home, it secretes a liquid that combines with the particle to eventually create a pearl. The pearl can live in the oyster's home for the rest of the oyster's natural life without causing any disturbance.

In the same way, rather than react negatively to people and events, we can include them and mould with them. Through acceptance, our consciousness jumps to another level of perception and we realise that what we might have previously regarded as a problem can, if handled correctly, be a means to develop our strengths and remove our weaknesses. Whether a situation is a problem or a gift depends on our perception. The choice is ours.

3

MEDITATION AS EDUCATION

SPIRITUAL EDUCATION LEADS us back to the understanding and the experience of our holistic existence as human beings, to the knowledge that we are spiritual, as well as physical, mental and emotional beings. Until the spiritual element is acknowledged, the compassion of human nature cannot be realised.

A true spiritual education could be described as:

> learning from others
> growing through others
> integrating with others
> contributing to others.

When we are genuinely learning, only then can we experience spiritual growth. When we grow, we integrate with others and it is in that integration that there is a natural and mutual contribution to the nature and being of each other. These four processes of education are constantly at work, but only happen in a way that is enjoyable and meaningful when the spiritual resources of the self are activated and creatively used.

These resources, in conjunction with the mind and intellect, enrich the way we see the world, the way we interact with it and the way we individually create our place in it. These resources are the original qualities of the self, which we have not properly used for a long time. With the awareness of our spiritual dimension, we start to harness and use these positive energies.

In order to initiate and further sustain this process we need faith in the self:

> Do I believe who I am?
> Do I believe what I have?
> Do I believe I can be more?

Our original resources are very simply - peace, love, purity, knowledge and happiness. In Raja Yoga meditation these are called the five original qualities of the soul. When we return our consciousness to these five qualities and remember them, then we can translate them as follows:

> Love: I care and I share.
> Peace: I harmonise and reconcile.
> Purity: I respect and I honour.
> Knowledge: I am and I exist.
> Happiness: I express and I enjoy.

To understand and remember these qualities, we need to recognise the heavy deep shadows which have blotted them out, or polluted them. Sometimes we don't recognise the pollutants because they have engrained themselves so deeply into the personality that we say, 'I am this.'

We do not realise that we are more than the limits we repeatedly place on ourselves.

What is it that limits and overshadows us? The prayers and the requests of the human race for many centuries. With 'I need', 'I want' and 'I own', people place value on the self by relating to the material, external aspects of their lives. However, this does not work and when people insist on behaving in this way (that is, relating to the outside), then addictive attachments are created. They try to fill themselves, but the exact opposite happens: the self becomes more and more empty. Unfortunately, the mechanism of need and greed functions in this way: first, there is the illusion of gain and secondly, when this is not realised, depletion, instead of enrichment, occurs. Whatever the addiction is, no matter how camouflaged it may be, it quietly but surely, ruins the person. It is a silent illness that only meditation can cure.

> *'I expect' is the great illusion, which converts itself into demanding rights without due respect for others.*

Anger in all its forms is a direct result of an expectation not being fulfilled and brings cries (albeit sometimes silent ones) of 'They should have done this', 'Why did this happen?' or 'Don't you know better?' Disappointment, accusations and demands are violent energies, which we throw around very naturally and easily in our daily life when our expectations are not fulfilled. They are like a burning fire that eats away at our original spiritual qualities, turning them to a dust that pollutes the self and others.

Instead, let us continue to practise returning our thoughts to the self and remembering our original source of peace. In that experience of deep, natural peace, we will find balance and clarity and the ability to tolerate and adjust to the unexpected.

One of the keys of meditation practice is to quickly gather our thought energy and take it inside to connect to our original qualities, no matter what may be happening outside, or even inside!

> *Let me disconnect from the external and plug in to the internal energies that support me.*

Meditation, in practice, means to enter, and re-enter, this reservoir of peace whenever we need to during the course of the day. This exercise increases self-control and prevents the explosions and reactions of anger that drain our strength. The easy method is not to expect but to accept: then tolerance and respect make our life a lot more comfortable.

There may be other shadows and pollutants, but usually our pain pivots on these: 'I own', 'I need', 'I want', 'mine' and 'I expect'. If we learn to recognise the characteristics of such a consciousness, we are in a position to diffuse difficult situations and thoughts before they overwhelm us. We simply have to remain awake, and that state of alertness stops these shadows from overpowering us and making us unconscious.

Our needs and wants are truly fulfilled in a healthy way by tuning in to the original resources of the soul, because their fulfilment is not dependent on anyone, or anything from outside. When we sustain ourselves from the inside, then our well-being is secure and progressive. As a result, when we express and show our original qualities of the self to others, whether it is peace, happiness or love, they naturally increase inside. The more we give unconditionally, the more we have. This miracle of 'quality being' is the consequence of natural purity, the original state of selflessness, which God always has and yogis aspire to return to.

4

TOUCHING THE CORE

MEDITATION IS AN attempt to find the true self. It is this self which holds the identity of what I am, an identity which, when realised, gives fulfilment and direction to our life. This is what we call the consciousness of 'I am', which emerges in meditation when there is concentration on the present and we focus on the now of 'I am', rather than the past, or the future ('I was', or 'I will be').

To remind us of this state, we use the word 'OM', which means 'I am a soul', the spiritual identity that acts as a key to human consciousness. As we find and realise the true self, we become aware of the false self and how deeply entrenched it is in our lives, both in our way of thinking and being.

When we understand this illusory self then we can begin the process of dissolving its negative effects on the original self.

The illusory self is made up of desires that, even when fulfilled, fail to add value, or a sense of worth to the self. In fact, quite the opposite process happens.

Let us examine some of these illusions and how they give us a mistaken sense of value.

Illusion	Thought	Result
Ego	I know, I am	arrogance, inflexibility, controlling others
Anger	I expect	force, aggression
Attachment	I own, It's mine	insecurity, possessiveness, jealousy
Greed	I want, I need	emptiness, wanting, dissatisfaction
Lust	I desire	exploitation, misuse, emotional dependence

These are the five fires that burn away the quality of human life: uncontrolled emotions that once, in their original pure state, gave happiness and peace to the individual but now create only emptiness and sorrow.

Ego

Identification with the ego and the external creates a false identity and extremes of feeling inferior, or superior, depending on the circumstances and people. It brings with it the thought of 'I am', which is based on gender, religion, nationality, achievement or talent, creating an attachment to the self, which always compares and competes with others. This insecurity leads a person into compelling others to act and think in the same way. Difference is measured as a threat, rather than as an innate gift with a right to expression.

Where there is such ego, only 'yes' people are allowed to come close: anyone with a difference of opinion is rejected. With ego, the original uniqueness of the self is denied, unrecognised and buried deep in the layers of wrong identity. This is why, these days, there is such an identity crisis – humanity has lost its soul, or rather, sold its soul to external 'quick fixes', traditions and attractions.

With ego, there is the idea of 'I know best' and consequently the misconceived duty and right to control and manipulate others, in their best interests! This has resulted in dogmas and laws, which fossilize the creativity and uniqueness of others.

'Who am I?' and 'What am I?' are questions whose answers lie in the recognition of our inner values and those resources being used in life. When individual human beings find their spiritual identity again, then they adopt the true values of the self, the true being, that cannot be invented or created; they are there all the time but we simply have to remember them.

Through meditation, the pollution of the selfish ego is gradually replaced by the remembrance and the experience of the pure self: the 'I' that is not attached to anything, or anyone, but is completely whole within itself. The expression of this pure entity is not selfish but selfless and the person begins to share - where necessary, facilitating the awakening of the true potential of others, just like sunlight. Light is a great facilitator. It steps in, awakens and moves on. An egoless person acts, interacts and expresses themselves in this way.

Anger

It is easy to understand how anger is one of the greatest fires in the human mind. Anger may take the form of yelling, shouting and verbal abuse, such as threatening, accusing, demanding, giving ultimatums: 'Do it or else!' But anger is also seen in the irritation when we do not speak: it is that silent smouldering where we emit fumes and fires of stored resentments and indignation, which effectively cuts real communication with others and ultimately ruins relationships. We get angry because we expect a certain type of behaviour from someone and when it is not forthcoming we become violent, convincing ourselves that others deserve to be punished. However, this result is an unresolved violence, which keeps emerging according to time and circumstance. Angry people feel too self-justified to even contemplate forgiveness, or letting go, in order to pacify a person or situation – they are too attached to their sense of being right and the other wrong.

In its original form, anger was not anger, not a negative reaction; rather it was the energy of a positive response to people and situations, but the response gave way to reaction. When we return to our spiritual identity, we begin to rediscover that capacity to be still, or centred, and we are then able to respond positively even to negative situations, or people. With spiritual consciousness, the energy of this response is transformed into being able to accept, understand and deal wisely and peacefully with whoever, or whatever, is encountered.

Attachment

Influenced by the ego, the original power of pure love changes its expression to attachment. In this stage of attachment, we find ourselves trying to possess others or to find an identity through them. In the name of love, we glue ourselves to other people, to roles, to positions, striving to find a sense of security and support. However, because these things are external, there is the underlying fear of loss and this creates more clinging, jealousy and possessiveness.

Greed

When we turn to the motive and false assumption behind greed, we recognise the thought and feeling that 'the more I have, the more I am'. It is a combination of trying to add to the value of the self through material possessions, position, role, talent, or achievements and then becoming attached to these as a form of identity, inevitably leading to personal collapse. To try to add to the sense of self in this way has the effect of detracting from the real self, which is why, in many cases, a person who has everything material is left with the feeling of being empty, disorientated and even fearful.

We cannot accumulate, or rely on the external, to create a sense of personal value.

People often try to fill the void of personal inadequacy through greed, but this 'method' goes against natural, universal laws. All that I am, all that I can be, all that will make me truly happy must begin from inside the self. We have to start from the inside out, not the other way round, otherwise we create desires that have no end, like the seven-headed monster guarding the Golden Fleece: every time Jason, the hero, cut off one head, another grew in its place. The monster did not die until he aimed for the heart. Desires are created from wanting one thing or another, believing that we will find achievement when those desires are fulfilled. This pattern of behaviour keeps deceiving us and the proof of this is seen in the state of discontentment and emptiness people find themselves in.

Lust

The desire that many find most difficult to understand is that of lust. This is manifested when the procreative power of the human soul becomes a selfish fire that burns away self-respect and respect for others. People have begun to accept this type of desire as normal, to believe that they may give in to this desire at any time, forgetting that inner qualities like loyalty, patience and the willingness to grow and learn with another is the basis for a relationship. The undisciplined use of this procreative energy indicates a deep selfishness, which creates and sustains an emotional dependence that damages and often destroys self-value and the spiritual meaning of respectful relationships.

In Raja Yoga meditation these five diseases of the soul are known as Maya, which means illusion, a deception of the self in pursuing wrong ways to achieve happiness. The human soul has the capacity to follow this path of illusion, or to choose a way of life that is more positive and fulfilling. The choice depends on the degree to which the soul recognises these five diseases and their progeny and transforms them.

Having recognised the weaknesses, what is the medicine to bring the soul back to a state of good health?

To conquer *ego*, humility and honesty are required. We need the courage to look into the self honestly and acknowledge that the characteristics of 'I know' and 'I control' exist and have to be removed, if there is to be truth and happiness. We need to remember the original 'I am', what we call 'Om Shanti' consciousness.

I am a peaceful, spiritual being; this is my true identity.

In order to extinguish *anger*, one has to use peace and silence, to understand that peace is the original state of one's being, to remember that 'I am a peaceful being' means to emerge the consciousness of non-violence. Silence, that is learning to put a break on the mind and tongue, helps us to think before speaking and, consequently, saves us from many confrontations with others.

To overcome *attachment*, there needs to be detachment, that is, a space between myself and my violent emotions, desires and needs, and between myself and others. We need to create a respectful space; to understand that we do not progress or find our self through others. When we free the self from such a state, then we find our true self and experience a spiritual independence that is kind, loving and embracing towards others, but simultaneously beyond dependence.

To fill the space created by *greed*, let the soul understand the power of true generosity. The act of repeatedly taking is a disease of selfish need that becomes such a habit that the soul thinks it is normal, especially in relationship with other people. Though it may have become normal, it is *not* natural; the proof of this is the pain, sorrow and discontentment experienced in most people's lives.

Generosity means to give to the self by recognising the original spiritual qualities of the self, emerging them and naturally sharing them with others.

To diminish the fire of *lust*, let the soul use the medicine of respect. Where there is a genuine respect for the other, there will not be exploitation of emotions. With respect, balance and harmony cool the senses and the spirit. There is a caring that truly takes into consideration the existence of the other as an independent and valuable being, not to be misused emotionally or physically by being self-centred.

Raja Yoga means to become the king of the self.

It is through this inner conquest that we are able to recognise and use our immortal resources, or medicine. Often, if we cannot unlock or recognise this inner medicine, then the connection with the Supreme Source of energy is necessary. Meditation is the connection with God, which releases these positive energies in the self.

5

THE INVISIBLE FACTOR

THE MOST POWERFUL things are invisible. For example, the roots of a tree cannot be seen; they are underground silently nurturing the visible tree. A house is supported by its foundation deep within the earth; if the foundation is weak, the building will fall when there is some kind of strong pressure, like an earthquake. The essence of matter is the atom; it holds a tremendous amount of energy but cannot be seen by the eyes.

Can we see God? I have not met anyone who has seen Him. People have experienced, or felt God's presence but no one has actually seen a personal form, yet millions believe in such a Being! In the same way, when it comes to knowing the true self, we ask, 'What does the soul look like? Where is it situated?'

A human being is soul and body, spirit and matter, working together co-operatively. The body is like the hardware of a computer and the spiritual energy, the soul, is a tiny chip of light, where all things are recorded; the full programme of the soul is there. When we go into introspective silence, it is in this chip of light, which is actually a point of light energy, that we can remember and rediscover.

The tiny chip of invisible light starts to work effectively when it plugs into its original consciousness and reactivates those original qualities, which enable the soul to work and express itself naturally. The connection is achieved through the power of concentrated thought; this is called 'consciousness of the soul'. The process of experiencing 'soul consciousness' is carried out in meditation: gathering all the thoughts of the mind, creating one concentrated thought and very gently turning inwards in order to make the connection with the original self, the soul.

To take those first steps in gathering the thoughts, we use the positive consciousness of 'I am', or what is called 'Om Shanti' consciousness. 'Om' means 'I am', with the deeper meaning that 'I am a soul'. With this awareness, there comes the experience of one's original spiritual identity.

The soul has five primary qualities; we could say they are the primary colours of our humanity with which we paint the picture of our lives. They are:

Peace
This is the original quality of the soul. Peace is serenity, the personal inner state of non-violence. In this state of peace, I harmonise with everything and everyone around me. The word 'shanti' means peace, and it is this thought we use as the key step in meditation.

Purity
A state of honesty and cleanliness where I am the same inside and outside, not deceiving either myself, or others. Consequently, there is no room for artificiality. Purity is the state of original truth where no violence is committed against others, nor can violence be perpetrated against me. When the self is in its original purity, others cannot damage or destroy it, even if they try, because there is a natural aura of protection that acts as an invisible barrier. When I achieve this level of purity, it means I respect all things.

Love
Perhaps the most difficult original quality to achieve because it has become so mixed up with attachment, possessiveness

and dependence, deeply engrained habits that have become accepted as normal. As a result, the human being finds it difficult to realise the true form of pure love, which is unconditional. The quality of love means "I care", I share and, in particular, I liberate. True spiritual love never creates that need, or dependence, where others cannot find, or be, themselves. Love is the greatest power and blessing in the Universe.

Knowledge

To know and to be what I am eternally and truly, and to exist in this consciousness, is what is meant by knowledge. It is not knowing *about* the soul, peace, love, etc., but rather knowing is to *be* the soul, to *be* peace, to *be* love. This quality of true knowing is expressed through 'I am', the original awareness of the self that exists beyond the false self of ego.

Happiness

Happiness is the natural expression of joy in being alive and interacting with others. Happiness is only possible when I relate to myself and express respectfully what I am and allow others to share in what I am and what I have. I relate to people and nature and experience the fulfilment of human life through relationship.

As we become aware of these five primary qualities, we gradually realise that each one of them has many characteristics.

For example, we understand that love does not mean just a special feeling for one or two people. Spiritual love is far greater; it means respect, tolerance, forgiveness, compassion and flexibility; there is a universal feeling of belonging, an openness of heart, a generosity of spirit that is all-embracing.

Learning to Meditate

If we do not exercise or use the muscles of our legs for a long time, it will be difficult to use them to walk. This is what has happened to the human spirit. The legs of the mind and intellect have not been exercised spiritually for a long time and so they have become unhealthy: there is no permanent peace, happiness or contentment. We have exercised ourselves intellectually by analysing, discussing and accumulating information, etc., but the spiritual dimension has been missing. This has resulted in the soul remaining underdeveloped and undernourished, a real poverty of spirit, which is reflected in the crises that are happening everywhere, both personally and globally.

So, meditation is that spiritual exercise which revives the original qualities of the human soul, bringing them back into our awareness.

Step 1. Sit in a comfortable and relaxed position. There is no need for a special position, but you need a balance between being too comfortable (in which case it is easy to fall asleep) or too rigid (in this case it is possible that you will begin to feel tense, physically and mentally). Keep the eyes open a little as this helps; to stay awake; gently concentrate on the third eye.

Step 2. Concentrate your attention on the centre of the forehead. Visualise a point of energy. This point of light is the 'Om'.

I am the spiritual identity working within this physical body, my material instrument, but I am not this body. I truly am this tiny point of spiritual energy.

Step 3. Focus on the thoughts:

I am a soul, a spiritual being. I am a point of energy that is eternal and ultimately beyond time, sound and matter.

Step 4. Take your thoughts deeper into your inner world. Discover and begin to experience your original strength of peace.

My original strength and original quality is peace.

Step 5. Ask yourself *'What is peace?'* When we examine what it is, then this understanding makes it easy for concentration to take place. If we do not exercise this word in our mind and intellect, it cannot be ingested. Otherwise, we know of the idea of peace but it remains just an intellectual idea, rather than a personal reality or experience.

Peace has a number of synonyms, which all have slightly different shades of meaning:

Serenity
The feeling of contentment and being completely full with no need for further additions to the self; a feeling of satisfaction, of wholeness of the self.

Calmness
There are no disturbances or waves in the mind, like a pool of water that is clear and still with not even a ripple to disturb it.

Tranquillity

Here is the state of harmony in nature and in ourselves that keeps everything in balance naturally.

Quietness

In this state, there are no sounds of uncontrolled thoughts jumping around like a monkey in the mind; our thoughts become essenceful, returning to the point, with no expansion; it is an economy of thinking that creates quietness.

Stillness

There is no movement of thoughts. I remain absorbed in one thought and, in the stillness of silence, I am at rest, with a feeling of complete detachment from everything.

Peace has the meaning of harmony, balance, order and freedom: when we are free from waste and negativity, then we exist fully serene, fully at peace with everything.

> *Peace is my original energy and treasure and with concentrated thought I step inside and experience it.*

When we create a thought, it is usually expressed through words and action. However, during meditation, the thought is held in the mind and channelled inwards; such concentrated thought becomes like a key that opens up our inner spiritual reservoir.

Now, let's do a meditation exercise:

> *I sit relaxed and concentrate on the centre of my forehead, very slowly creating thoughts of peace.*

(It is important when meditating not to go too quickly, rather to be slow - the slowness allows for depth and ease. Relax the body in a comfortable position and gently, very gently concentrate on the centre of the forehead).

Continue with these thoughts:

> *'I relax. Slowly I relax. I concentrate on the centre of my forehead. I am calm. I begin my journey inward – my journey into silence. In this silence, the mind concentrates on one thought – the thought of the original self, the spiritual self.*

> *Who am I? ... Gently, I begin to experience the eternal being within. ... Om ... I am. ... I am a spiritual being, ... a soul; ... shanti, ... a being of peace. ... Peace is my original strength. ... I, the soul, ... a point of eternal*

energy, … I am the essence of peace. … Peace is harmony. … Peace is balance. … Peace is serenity. … Content, … complete, … full. … As my thought, so my consciousness. … Let me remain in this thought: … Om shanti. … Peace and silence. … Peace and silence. … I remain still. … I focus on myself, … as a point of eternal energy. … I, the soul, … a being of peace, … a being of serenity. … I remain still. … I remain in complete peace: … Om shanti.

Remember to do this exercise slowly, giving yourself time when you are not in a hurry. The mind and thoughts may go in other directions, but gently re-focus them, to realise the 'Om Shanti' consciousness, the original consciousness of peace.

Like learning a language, meditation requires systematic and patient practice on a daily basis to receive true benefit. If it is only done once in a while, or only in a state of need, then the state of being peaceful is not easily achieved. Rarely is anything learnt, or mastered, immediately. Therefore, it is important not to give up even if it does not seem to work. Just keep trying and gradually it comes by itself. Set aside 15 minutes in the morning and in the evening to practise this; as it becomes easier to do then you can increase the amount of time.

6

THE INNER EYE

PEOPLE HAVE ALWAYS been intrigued by the concept of the 'third eye'. What is it? Can it be opened during an operation, or by going to places like Tibet or India?! In meditation, we understand that the 'third eye' means the ability to understand and to perceive correctly, then, on the basis of that perception or insight, to act and behave accordingly. In other words, on the basis of spiritual truths, we think, speak and act so that peace and well-being become natural in our life.

> *Spiritual values, or truths, are necessary for genuine improvement of the human condition.*

The third eye is the intellect of the soul; when it is open, there is realisation of the need to improve, change and/or create something that will help the self and others to sustain a better quality life.

The soul has three faculties: the mind through which we create thoughts, the intellect with which we understand, discern and decide, and the sanskars, which are impressions in the form of memories, personality characteristics and habits. All three work together: the mind is influenced by both external and internal factors, which can be either positive or negative. The intellect has to understand, discern and decide what something means and then act. If the intellect is unclear or confused, then understanding and decisions are faulty and, consequently, actions and behaviour result in a lot of negativity, both for the self and others.

Throughout history, teachers have come to give spiritual knowledge, through which they attempt to awaken people's consciousness in order to make relationships, attitudes, thoughts and actions more positive and loving. For this to happen, there has to be a 'click' in the intellect, that is, a realisation and willingness to change old habits and negative personality characteristics and to become a better human being, ethically and spiritually.

Change is the result of the third eye opening.

In English, there is the word 'scope': a wide range of things that can be done, or understood. According to Chamber's *Essential English Dictionary*, 'If there is scope for something in a particular set of circumstances, there is freedom, or the opportunity to act in a certain way.' When the 'third eye' opens, its scope becomes broader and then there is greater possibility to think and act in a more positive way.

Our intellect has become dwarfed by ego, attachments, fear, stress, worry and greed, to name but a few of our subtle obstacles. However, as we begin to use the wider 'scopes' of the third eye in meditation, we are gradually released from a narrow way of thinking and from focusing unduly on wrong things; the more we open up on a subtle level, the more positive and beneficial becomes our focus.

What kind of 'scopes' are there?

There are telescopes, microscopes, periscopes, stethoscopes and kaleidoscopes. When the intellect is used with a variety of 'scopes', then its understanding adapts to the situations it observes. It understands clearly what something really means and then it discerns what is required for that situation, person, or self and acts accordingly. For any of the 'scopes' to work, we need spiritual knowledge, as well as meditation. Spiritual knowledge, which is the foundation of any meditation technique, lubricates the intellect and gives it the ability to focus in a variety of ways for a variety of purposes.

Let us take a closer look at the types of 'scope' and their impact on our vision:

Telescope

When the intellect, or third eye, is used in this way, it is able to understand the reality of 'consequence'. Every thought, every word and every action is like a planted seed that, in time, will bear fruit. When there is realisation of this reality, then there is attention paid to how we think, speak and act. We realise the importance of our own responsibility in creating certain situations, in creating our own attitude and state of mind; there is greater care and a more responsible use of our own power of choice.

> *With telescopic vision, we become the knower of the three aspects of time.*

In Raja Yoga, this is called being 'trikaldarshi', which literally means having the 'vision of the three aspects of time' in the sense that in the present I can learn from the past and create my future. The past cannot be changed, but my attitude to what has happened can be changed. Therefore, rather than having regret or bitterness, I understand the lesson of life and move on.

Microscope

When the lens of the intellect becomes refined, it is able to examine many things in detail. In the same way that a microscope is able to detect bacteria and the types of germ that cause particular types of disease, so too the intellect is able to use its microscopic capacity to detect those germs that cause emotional and spiritual illness. For example, it is able to examine and understand that the illness of anger comes from the germ of expectation, that the illness of possessiveness comes from the germ of insecurity, the illness of aggression, or forcefulness, comes from the germ of fear and that the illness of stress stems from the germs of worry, doubt and greed. If the germs are seen and understood, then the illness can be cured through the application of appropriate knowledge and meditation.

> *Meditation, in the form of a focused silence, acts like a spiritual laser dissolving the acquired germs and emerging the original healing energies of the self, such as peace and self-respect.*

Without this focused silence, it is difficult to remove the germs, even if they are seen and understood. The original innate energy of the soul is needed for any permanent cure.

Periscope

This is the ability of the intellect to come out, observe, understand and initiate appropriate action and, when necessary, go back inside and be calm and still. This act of taking the thoughts inside is called introspection and in this introspective state the self can re-energise, examine, reflect and refine, or just be completely still – whatever it may wish to do in that state of silence. When the intellect uses its capacity as a periscope, it is able to find a balance between the inside and outside worlds.

> *Effective meditation means to gather the positive resources of the inner self and then use them in the outer world.*

It is important to remain neither too much inside, nor too much outside, but constantly to create a balance between the inner and outer realities. Meditation resembles the cyclic path of energy: going from the inside out and then from the outside in, gathering information, or experiences that we need to reflect on, or understand better. On other occasions, it may be a question of recharging our minds with positivity and peace: we go inside and, with the practice of silence, the battery becomes re-energised.

Stethoscope

This is when the intellect is so sensitively focused that it can recognise the realities behind appearances. Sometimes we call this intuition. To be intuitive often means that the third eye is able to tune in to the hidden silent vibrations of other people and situations. Vibrations are energies, which are constantly being transmitted by all things, particularly living things and people. A person may not say anything, or may even say the opposite of what he or she is feeling, but we are able to understand this contradiction, either through facial expressions, or body language, or by picking up the thoughts.

The doctor uses the stethoscope to 'hear' the body of the patient and to examine and understand the pulse and rhythm of the body in order to gauge the health of the person; it is like a third ear!

If the intellect wishes to understand the pulse of another person, in order to truly cooperate and help properly, then it has to have the capacity of a third ear, which means developing the art of really listening and catching the needs of the situation and person. When the intellect is used like a stethoscope, it needs to be very introspective, very concentrated and very open. In this way, the intellect is used like a third eye and a third ear; seeing and listening become the same thing and such perception brings creative and constructive assistance to the many illnesses that now plague the human spirit.

Kaleidoscope

A kaleidoscope creates beautiful patterns from chaotic bits and pieces, which are scattered everywhere; when the kaleidoscope is turned, disorder becomes order, chaos becomes beauty and symmetry. The drama of life is constantly turning and we are part of its cyclic movement; sometimes this cyclic movement of life is supportive, comprehensible and enjoyable and, at other times, it is tense, fearful, stressful and incomprehensible. There is confusion and fear because we do not understand what is happening, why it is happening and how it will get better. Things not only appear chaotic but also hopeless. If the intellect is able to go beyond the questions of 'Why?', 'What?' and 'How?' and just be still, without judgements, or pressure, for some period of time, then things do work out. To do this requires faith.

> *The power of faith means that we know that somehow and somewhere right solutions and answers will come in their own time.*

We are so used to controlling people and situations to obtain a particular result that we have forgotten how to use this power of faith.

Faith says, 'Plant the right seeds, make the right effort, but also let things be.' Faith does not mean to be passive but rather to have acted and thought about something and then have the patience and trust that the Drama of Life is also taking care of it; the outcome of any action is not just up to me.

In Raja Yoga meditation, we often hear the term 'a faithful intellect is victorious'. As the Drama of Life turns, such an intellect works like a kaleidoscope and can perceive the often hidden, beautiful patterns that, in time, become visible and benevolent.

> *Success, or victory, depends as much on doing the task with the right intention, as it does on allowing things to take their own course. Wisdom is an awareness of this balance.*

7

KNOWLEDGE AND TRUTH

THE FIRST STEP into experience, particularly the meditation experience, is knowledge. What does it mean to 'know'? Knowing involves four steps, which ultimately give the meditator the experience of realization:

The first step of knowing is **information**. With information, our intellect opens to new ideas and opinions. To be properly informed, we need to listen carefully.

The second step of knowing is **knowledge**, when we begin to reflect and think on the ideas and views that we have listened to. At this point, we often have to select only a few of the ideas we have heard, as it is not always feasible to reflect on all the information that is fed to us. In order to deepen our understanding, we reflect on the information and sometimes discuss our findings and thoughts with others.

The third step of knowing is when we move from thinking to **doing**, that is, from knowledge to wisdom. Wisdom is gained when we commit ourselves to 'doing'. Knowledge translated into our everyday behaviour is called wisdom, which, in turn, is called quality life. A life of quality is where personal values are not only realised but also lived and experienced through our practical actions.

Doing, or practice, naturally brings us to the fourth and final step of knowing, which is called **Truth**.

> *Truth is 'to be': the pure state of being where nothing needs to be added, where nothing can be subtracted.*

For a human being, this takes a long time and a variety of processes. It is the ultimate state of consciousness that yogis and meditators aspire to. (This is often referred to as the consciousness of 'OM'.) It is said that God is eternally in this state of Truth. 'Om' is the consciousness of 'I am', the consciousness, which denotes both an uncreated selfhood and a pure state of being. The human soul originally had this consciousness of 'Om', but gradually forgot it. Therefore, the aim of 'knowing' (at least, spiritual knowing) is to return to this original state. The way of return is called 'remembrance', that is, to pay attention and keep remembering the eternity of the self, otherwise referred to as the soul, the *atma*.

On a spiritual path, we always need these four steps, but there is the great temptation for the majority of people to stay on the first two, which involve listening and thinking. Without a systematic and consistent commitment to personal action, we just develop the art of conceptualising, philosophising and discussing. Moreover, without practice and silence, we cannot develop the inner strength that is so vital for everyday life.

> *One aim of meditation is to develop inner strength through attention to practice.*

Practice is to observe and to take the opportunity to transform knowledge into an experience that helps us in our daily life.

One aspect is the practice of values such as tolerance, patience and flexibility. Another is for the meditator actually to experience the highest level of consciousness. It is said that when this highest level of consciousness is experienced, there is the strength to practice those values that create well-being.

How can we go beyond these stages of information, knowledge and even wisdom to experience the original state of being, that is, truth?

One way to describe the process is to compare it to the game of the pole-vaulter. The pole-vaulter has a long pole to help jump over the barrier. The athlete runs for a short distance, and then quickly fixes the pole into the ground, enabling the body to be lifted up. When the athlete reaches a certain point in the air, the very pole that was used to get to that point is discarded; if the athlete fails to let go of the pole, then the body will be propelled backwards and it will be impossible to accomplish the task of jumping over the barrier.

The same mechanism is involved when a person wishes to attain realisation of the self and an experience of a higher state of consciousness. To experience realisation, we have to run some distance, collecting the necessary information. Then we use the pole of knowledge and wisdom to lift us off the ground of ordinary consciousness. But, we must then let go of the very knowledge that we used to elevate our minds and take a jump of faith, flying over the barrier of 'ordinary consciousness' to experience a new and higher level of consciousness. If there is no faith, then there is not enough trust to let go and jump.

Many people do not let go of the pole of knowledge and, as a result, fall into the spinning of speculation and the habit of analysis and discussion - the experience of spiritual consciousness eludes them. The pull of the ego draws the consciousness back to the ground. The irony is that they think they have jumped over the barrier and regard themselves as being in the privileged position of knowing. Then they think that from this privileged position they have the prerogative of judging and being better than those who 'know' in a different way.

The ones who have let go of the pole can be characterised by their wider, creative perspective and their benevolent strength.

Ultimately, true knowing is a state of positive being and its most powerful experience and expression is in silence.

8

THE POWER OF SILENCE

IT SEEMS CONTRADICTORY to speak, or write, about silence because silence is really something to be experienced. In the experience of silence, we discover deep spiritual truths and come to know our spiritual self. Silence grows within us, helping us to progress and develop in a very subtle way, just like a seed: the flower is hidden in the seed, the seed is hidden in the earth. Sunlight touches the earth that warms the seed and the flower begins to grow. Like a seed, we are also full of a great deal of potential. It is not really knowledge, or discussion, that will truly develop that potential. They help, of course, but it is the light of silence that penetrates very deeply and awakens the potential within, inspiring it to burst into flower. Silence is also a space that gives the mind oxygen, allowing the creation of something new, filling life with power and strength.

Everybody's religion nowadays is one of being busy. Everyone rushes around, doing something, proving something, showing something. In that rush to be someone, we tend to forget the great power and miracle found in stillness.

> *One aspect of meditation is that it teaches us to face life from the inside.*

It takes us to that point of stillness where we find the strength to change and heal the inner self. In that silence, we are able to find perspective and insight. In a deep state of introspection, we clearly observe our thoughts, seeing our true motives; when we understand that our intentions are perhaps not quite right, then we are in a position to say to ourselves, 'Hold on a minute!'

When we use silence to check our thoughts at that level, then we begin to realise that many of the things we are thinking about are not really worth thinking about. At this point, we become spiritually economical, which in fact leads us to becoming very generous. A lot of precious energy is lost, both mentally and emotionally, on wasteful and negative thinking. Ninety-five percent of our time is wasted on thinking about others; we go on and on with a string of expectations, which becomes like a hammer of demand on other people's heads.

Take a combination of expectations and demand, and what does it equal? Conflict!

> *When we learn to become silent and to reflect on our inner self, we start feeling satisfied with what we find inside and there is a deep sense of contentment.*

We become more compassionate in our outlook and start accepting others for who they are. The more we are able to accept, the sooner we find that there is harmony in our relationships. We start saving energy, sparing our thoughts and our words. This is accompanied by more patience, tolerance, flexibility, easiness and lightness. Silence teaches us the art of living. Silence can be misused to isolate oneself, but true, positive silence gives us a balance between our inner and outer worlds. Having explored our inner self, we collect our positive energy, become aware of our qualities, and then very naturally these are expressed externally. We move our concentration to the inner self and then to the external world. Then we go inwards again. It is a circular movement. As we go into silence, we recharge our inner energies, become one with the self, heal our self, relax and release our self from negativity. There are so many benefits by simply stepping inside to meet our true self. As we draw out these riches and resources, what do we do with them? We share them and give them out and in doing this we receive and we learn.

Silence is the guiding light that helps us to find a balance between inner and outer expression.

Too much silence is not good. We need to go in, discover, and then come out and share. If we only stay inside, we can lose our self. We can become uncaring about others. That is not a healthy silence. Then again, you get those who always remain with the external. They spend all their time criticizing, analysing, discussing, examining and rushing around. They cannot be still for even a few moments.

One of the methods we use in Raj Yoga is called 'Traffic Control'. This method consists of being still for a few moments, stopping the traffic of our thoughts. Stepping back, we free the self from tension. We look at the picture of where we are going and then go back into whatever activity we were involved in. However, going into that silence actually helps us to be more effective and grounded. This is a very useful method, particularly when practised a few times a day.

Meditation actually helps us to discover our real self.

This is something that most people have a problem with nowadays; they don't know who exactly they are, or where they are going, or why they are here. They lead a very robotic existence (eating, sleeping, working, drinking, etc). Eventually, they get frustrated and break down. Unfortunately, in the world today, there are so many economic, social and political breakdowns. These arise from crises in people, due to the diminishing prominence of values in everyday life.   Moreover, people have such misplaced values: wanting, needing, taking and comparing. All this takes them away from their simplicity and their naturalness. How can we help them to get back to their roots? By leading them to silence, to meditation.

The word 'meditation' comes from the Latin word 'meditari', which is a probable cognate of the word 'mederi' meaning 'to heal'. Journeying inside, discovering the inner self and our true power is the beginning of the healing process, in which we are able to put back all the broken pieces with a lot of love. Do I like, respect and love myself? In meditation, I reconcile myself to myself, I accept myself, I discover the uniqueness of my own being at this particular point in time. I also tune into those original resources of my spirit, which are simply love, peace, joy and happiness, to name but a few.

With patience and practice, we need to strengthen three aspects of our real self:

self-respect

self-esteem

self-confidence

Self-respect

This depends on knowing who I am, knowing my eternal, spiritual self. When I have found that sense of spiritual identity, I feel I have a right to be here, to exist. Without the spiritual dimension, it is very difficult to really respect myself deeply. In this case, I base my respect on identifying with the superficial aspects of my being: looks, gender, success, my spouse, my intelligence. With such superficial identification, I will never have a stable sense of self-respect, because people's opinions change. Today they love me, tomorrow they reject me. What is the consequence of depending on their opinions? I will end up fluctuating all the time – feeling positive when they say good things, and feeling down when they say negative things. To stay stable in my self-respect, I need to nurture a deeper understanding of my spiritual identity (the foundation of this being that I am a soul) and tap into those riches that are within me eternally, waiting to blossom, like the flower from the seed.

As I become grounded in such a spiritual awareness, those riches and resources start flowing out of me. The more stable

I am in my self-respect and spirituality, the more I emanate what I truly am. I feel a deep sense of contentment and I am happy to be me, however I am. I accept myself as I am. When I have no connection with my spiritual roots, I become dependent on others and, unfortunately, I sometimes mistake this dependence to be love when it is normally just a need, or an attachment. When this happens, the relationship doesn't work for long, because I have attached myself to someone, giving them neither space nor respect. They begin to feel suffocated because I have trespassed on their freedom and, eventually, the result of the whole relationship is a feeling of bondage. Only when the soul is in a state of complete self-respect, can there be freedom in relationships.

Self-esteem
Self-esteem comes when I really value myself. When I place value on myself, then others, too, will value me. When I don't value myself, how can I expect others to value me? If I continually put myself down, saying 'I'm no good' or 'I am not capable', other people who hear this will start believing it. So what do I do? The key word is 'consciousness'. As I start to become more conscious, more spiritually alert, then I am in a position to start valuing my life. The effect of this is that I start valuing others, understanding that everyone has their own position: not higher or lower, just different. Each one's

uniqueness has its value and when I recognise the value of the self, I develop self-confidence.

Self-confidence

Self-confidence is very much linked to the understanding that I definitely have something to contribute to life through my own uniqueness. Each one of us is unique. That goes without saying. Unless a person has a sense of contributing, or offering, something to life, they cannot really be happy. I cannot be happy when I am just taking; it simply doesn't work. I can only be happy when I am sharing and offering the best of myself. In that way, I don't feel depleted. When I offer the best of myself in an unselfish way, my happiness increases - the more I give, the more I receive. We start to understand that the well-being of individuals begins when they can contribute what they are, and what they have, to others. To be a true human being means to have true spiritual powers, like love, peace and happiness, that are brought into daily life – not just appearing as words or emotions, but truly manifesting themselves in behaviour.

For example, take the quality of love. It is not just a feeling of passion, the Hollywood type of love. It is much deeper; it is being able to say 'I learned from the past'; it is forgetting grievances; it is forgiveness. Rather than having animosity, or resentment, let me show compassion. The more I feel compassion, the more I love myself. Forgiveness is a wonderful medicine for me because it releases me from feeling bitter. It is also wonderful for the person I forgive. Hatred does not justify anything, nor does it release anyone from pain, or other negative emotions and feelings. Let me learn, forget and move on. This is a guaranteed therapy.

Love is just one example of the spiritual resources that are found within the self. By tapping into these resources, we become better human beings. It takes a little time to connect with the self in this way, but if we keep this aim clearly in front of us, we will be successful. Practising meditation helps us to reach our goals, because during meditation we link our soul self with the Supreme Energy, who fills us with power. The freer we become, the more confident we are with the ability to trust our self more. We become more stable in our own self, we are able to control our reactions a bit better and we wait. We don't suppress the self. Rather, we wait, observe, clarify and then control our reaction (including, of course, our tongue!).

As we start to do things more positively and compassionately, we start to grow in our own self-respect and self-confidence.

We don't want to be ruled by our negative emotions. We still meet them, acknowledge them, try to understand them and dissolve them. We cannot pretend that they are not there, but we are no longer a slave to the negative. As we follow our spiritual path more closely, we learn that we don't want to damage ourself, nor do we want to damage others. We become a little more careful. Sometimes we know what is the right thing to do, but still we are not able to control our reactions, or act correctly. We know, understand, agree but still can't do the right thing. Then we are filled with guilt and regret, having done the wrong thing. We lose our self-respect. What can we do then? Where do we find the strength to change? In silence.

In silence, we are able to find the strength to be able to put those values into practice. Silence is a great therapy for healing the self. If we remain very quiet and concentrate, we save a lot of outward energy, with the result that we act and speak less. When that energy is saved, then we are able to turn inwards and even heal our physical body.

On a daily basis, the mind needs to go into a quiet space for refreshment and reflection, in much the same way as the body needs regular breaks for rest and nourishment. Refreshment occurs when the mind is able to recharge itself, that is, to reenergize and to have the strength to remain positive, light and creative. Reflection is the time we give ourselves to refine our understanding so that our interaction with others is of the highest quality. Through reflection, we can change the way we think, feel and interact. We change the way we are voluntarily and without pain.

Knowledge without silence is like a bird trying to fly with only one wing.

Silence empowers an individual's capacities and enables the recognition and release of their unique potential. In today's world, silence is as necessary for the mind as oxygen is for the body. We need that spiritual breath that sustains our life in a way that is meaningful and fulfilling.

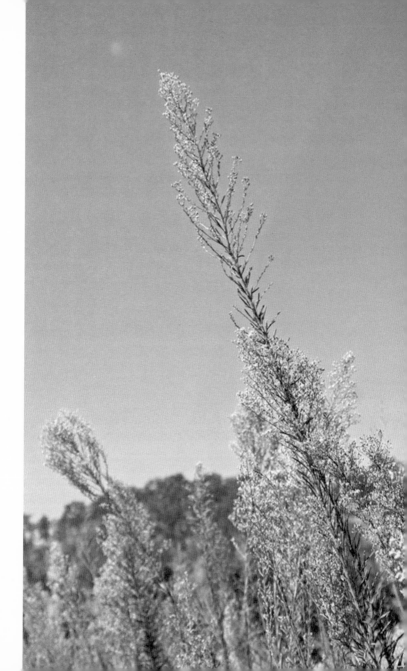

9

SEVEN STEPS INTO SILENCE

THE SEVEN STEPS of Silence are the complements, the bridges, or steps, that take us into the depths of knowledge, increase our core strength and release creative energy into the world, a contribution that not only can we all make, but which is of the utmost necessity.

Step One: Listening

People often speak of opening the third eye but our true step into deepening understanding is to open our third ear! What this means is to tune the self to understand what is really being said to me.

This requires that I create a stillness within, by detaching as far as possible from the conditionings of my personality, from myself and from my way of thinking, so as not to interpret new knowledge according to old patterns.

I need to step back from myself in order to listen to myself. Listening is creating that respectful space between myself and the other, which facilitates a real understanding of what the other is trying to say to me. Listening through the 'third ear' creates a link of empathy: an attentive calm and openness that focuses the mind so that reality can be grasped. Such attentive awareness enables the mind to create concentrated and pure thought. As Einstein said, 'I firmly believe, as the ancients believed, that pure thought can grasp reality.'

What is the reason for going into silence? Why would I want to tune my mind and attitude to listening?

As the world becomes more complex and problems become further intertwined, *listening is the first step to communicating and harmonising with everyone;* it is a method to understand the reality of the other in order to live better with them. Listening to myself, to God, to others and to nature enables the self to harmonise and to enjoy a sense of equilibrium.

Step Two: Reflection
Reflection is a necessary step in digesting knowledge, to show that I understand what I hear.

Reflection is an exercise of the mind and intellect that goes into the depths of understanding an idea, or realisation, with the intent of practising it in daily life.

Values in my life signal that knowledge has been digested; without this, knowledge simply remains a beautiful aspect, appreciated, interesting information in my intellect but without the ability to give me strength because it is still external; it has not been internalised.

All quality action, all newness of perception, all new insights, or vision, require a space for silent reflection as a preliminary step. Reflection is the springboard to dive into the pool of quality action.

Quality action is that action which is truly appropriate to person, circumstance and the need of the moment.

Normally, we are lost in the business of action, its routine and ritual that make our life so mechanistic and hence dull and boring, or demanding and hectic.

A mind and intellect that do not give time and attention to reflective silence become lazy, though externally there is lots of activity for hours and hours. No new heights are reached because there is no depth of awareness in what we are doing, no reflection on purpose, nor intention. As a result, we get trapped by routine.

To be dictated to by external situations, which make us run around without stopping internally, induces unnecessary stress on the mind, which keeps us tied to the strings of the external, like a puppet pulled, pressed and pushed by circumstances.

> *To break free from this force, to relieve the mind of the weight of stress and waste and routine, I need to step inside and reflect on who I am and where I am going and reassess my value system.*

Otherwise, life becomes like a wheel that keeps spinning faster and faster until we become dizzy - we want to get off but it is going so fast we do not know how.

Reflection and taking time to understand bring us to the essence of everything.

Step Three: Concentration

When we reflect properly, we start to be economical with our thought energy. When milk is churned, it is gradually reduced in volume until it becomes butter. When we have many ideas, or thoughts, about a particular thing and we reflect in the right way, those ideas start to become cleaner and clearer, that is, more essenceful.

Bringing our thoughts to the essence is called concentration.

Such concentration is natural and not forced. We cannot concentrate naturally unless we have been through the reflection process.

When the mind gets to that point of concentration where mental energy is conserved, then we are empowered. An inner spring of energy is opened, which flows through us and takes us up to another level of consciousness.

With some meditation techniques, people are given ideas or mantras, which they often simply repeat. They do not penetrate the mind bringing any sense of meaning. People bounce these ideas around like a ball in their mind and, from the mind, the ball of thought is bounced to the mouth. Sound patterns are repeated, but nothing has really been understood. The result of this is that there is no power generated from within to effect change in behaviour, or personality, so everything continues in the same way. In these cases, people are not focused on spirituality. Consequently, after a while, such people find meditation boring, they fall asleep, or think that by repeating words, either verbally or mentally, they are doing meditation. However, the right type of concentration is not brought about simply by the repetition of sounds or ideas.

> *Natural concentration is when the mind can hold a thought for a long time, when thoughts are under our own control.*

Without concentration the mind goes here, there and everywhere, jumping like a monkey from branch to branch, idea to idea. When there is a natural concentration, we master our mind and there is peace. This one-pointed concentration on a thought, holding it for as long as we like, gradually accumulates strength in the mind and in the self.

A strong mind is a mind that is peaceful, stable, contented and can remain in the essence of a thought. There is no waste caused by over-thinking, or speed of thought; these are the two greatest diseases of the mind these days, which is why there is so much stress and mental breakdown.

Step Four: Connection

Once we have mastered the art of concentration, we are able to experience the fourth step of meditation, which is connection. With our power of thought, we connect with our original feelings and state of peace. We plug in to our socket and feel the current and as we connect we experience the fifth step of silence.

Step Five: Absorption

The self is absorbed in spiritual peace. For this connection and absorption to take place, the thought cannot be distracted, otherwise a short circuit occurs and the energy flow stops because the thought has become disconnected from the socket.

> *If we refine our understanding of the fourth step, the connection in Raja Yoga meditation is not only with the original self but also with God.*

The human soul plugs into the unlimited pure energy reservoir of the Universe, often called God. This Being is in reserve throughout eternity, existing beyond time and matter. God is beyond the effect of pollution and decay which befalls every human soul. When we need to clean out our system, re-energise, or refill ourselves with power, we have to tap into that Reservoir and we can only do that through our thoughts.

> *If the thought is concentrated enough, the mind is able to transcend the ordinary, absorb the qualities of that Being and learn the meaning of inner excellence and liberation.*

Accordingly, we concentrate, connect and absorb pure energy into the self. The deeper the concentration, the greater the absorption in the self of the qualities radiated by God.

Step Six: Filling

As the self absorbs the energy of peace, or whatever positive energy it needs, it fills itself with that quality completely. If the concentration remains unbroken, then the absorption and filling happen quite naturally and automatically.

Step Seven: Donation

Donating is the final step of silence. We have filled the self with a particular quality and it starts flowing out of us. We allow this quality to touch the atmosphere around us and consciously donate this vibration to the world, enabling those in need to feel it and to absorb it.

> *This is the ultimate step of a true meditator, often referred to as the 'lighthouse' state.*

A lighthouse stands still and stable in one position and beams light all around. We are able to bring an original quality of the self into our consciousness, fill ourself with it and then, very naturally, let it radiate from the mind.

One of the most important aspects in this step of silence is the link with the Supreme Energy. We make this link with the Supreme Source, we absorb from that Source, we fill the self from that Source and then donate all that the Source has given us.

This is called 'angelic' or 'instrument' consciousness.

It is said that an angel is a human soul who has fallen so deeply in love with that Source of Light that it has transformed completely. It is totally filled with Light and Peace and its task is only to serve, to share Divine Love and Peace.

Let us practise the first three steps with an exercise in Raja yoga meditation.

1. I hold in my mind the words Om Shanti, 'I am a peaceful soul'. Let us reflect on this statement, or mantra. A mantra is something that frees the mind from wasteful and negative thoughts, stress and worry. A mantra is usually repeated over and over again in order to get the desired results. However, in meditation it is not a matter of repeating words over and over again without truly understanding them. Otherwise it becomes forced concentration. Concentration of the mind should be natural because, when it is, the mind can remain in a state of peace and relaxation for a very long time. The consequence of this is a recharging of the battery of the self, a renewal of energy from inside.

How do we achieve this state of natural concentration on the thought, 'I am a spiritual being', 'I am a peaceful being'?

2. I reflect on 'OM', the consciousness of 'I am'.
What does 'I am' mean? In this thought, the attention is drawn only to the present moment. I have no need to go into 'I was', 'I will be', 'I hope to be' or 'I should be'. To go deep into the self, *I need to be completely in the present.* This thought of 'I am' takes me into the consciousness of self-realisation.

3. I focus and concentrate on the thought until I stop thinking about it and **experience** *it.*

These first three steps of silence are the most important and once mastered correctly, the other four steps follow on very easily.

10

CONNECTING WITH
THE DIVINE

PLATO ONCE SAID that true knowledge is to remember what you have forgotten. Truth actually means not to forget that the human soul carries within itself all the knowledge and resources it needs to lead a happier life.

In Raja Yoga meditation the word 'remembrance' is used, rather than 'yoga' or 'meditation', to describe what meditation actually means and does. Meditation that empowers the self by giving peace to the mind, clarity to the intellect and positive change to the personality is not achieved simply through ritual, or a repetition of words with little, if any, understanding. Rather, it is achieved by understanding what the words mean, reflecting on the ideas behind them and, with concentration bringing them actively into our consciousness. When the consciousness has that enlightened awareness, then the next step is action. We emerge our original state of peace, of knowing, of love, not just for ourselves but to use and share in daily life.

We cannot experience spiritual powers and values until we understand what they mean and where they come from and decide to apply them in our life.

> *Understanding and application are the basis of self-realisation and positive living.*

Of course, what happens is that sometimes we do understand and even apply our values but, because of the pressures and distractions of life, we forget to apply them consistently or systematically. This is why we need to revise and refresh our understanding and awareness through the practice of meditation every day, especially in the early morning.

How often do we breathe? How often do we eat and drink? To stay alive, these practices must happen consistently and systematically. This principle also applies to spiritual well-being. I cannot maintain my spiritual health unless, on a daily basis, I connect with myself and remember who I am and what I have within myself, recharging the self in the depths of silence.

Each morning before I start the journey of the day, to sit in silence, to reflect, to concentrate and to experience the consciousness of 'Om Shanti' recharges the self for the whole day. When I remember my original state of peace and inner harmony, my mind and intellect create an oasis of stability within, which helps me to face any storms of negativity that arise during the day.

To keep remembering our spiritual identity and our spiritual resources is challenging. Again and again, we need to remember and to return to our essence, our worth and our original strength. The words 'Om Shanti' help us to remember all of this when spoken gently and slowly in the mind, they become a key to open up our spiritual and human resources.

During the day we can stop for some moments to reflect and remember to be peaceful and silent. This act of stopping is like putting a brake on the mind.

I observe in what direction my thoughts, words and actions are going and then, if necessary, redirect or keep moving in the same direction with more clarity and focus.

This practice of remembrance is called 'traffic control'. It is a means to refresh, recharge and reorientate. When we forget to stop, the traffic of the mind becomes heavy and the driving tense, tiring, stressful and irritating and our mind and nerves seem ready to explode! To prevent all explosions and emotional eruptions, which ultimately destroy or damage our effectiveness, we need to stop. This is one practical use of remembrance.

On a deeper level, remembrance also means to connect the heart and mind to the Supreme Energy Source of the Universe. Through this connection the self is not only re-energised but also liberated from the repetitive patterns of wasteful thoughts and behaviours.

Sometimes one has the best intentions, the sincerest determination to eliminate certain habits but after a while these habits return. We feel trapped, we feel we cannot do what we would like to do and so we lose hope, or even the will to try again. The link with the Supreme Source of Energy gives the self the power to change, to dissolve and to finish negative patterns.

This link, which is possible when there is attention filled with love, enables a current of pure energy to reach the self. Through this spiritual current it becomes easier to stabilise in a positive state because this energy creates permanent changes.

> *When I remember the One, then the memory of my own state of original being returns and this memory creates the aim to return and rediscover those forgotten, or half-forgotten, qualities of the original being.*

The Supreme Source has the power to remind us of what we were because His original state of being is permanent; He never forgets Himself, is never polluted and remains eternally true to Himself in the state of spiritual, or soul, consciousness. As a result, He is the blueprint of what we were, of what we are to become. Very simply, the qualities of peace, love, purity, happiness and truth are there in Him, visible and available to those who wish to tune in and receive.

> *What we remember, we become, and so it is important to remember the right things. Number one on the list is thoughts of the original self and the Supreme Source.*

Imagine two points of light: one here on the earth, in time and matter, and the other beyond the earth, in another world of silence and peace. When these two points connect through the power of thought and feeling there is a union, which allows for a flow of energy and the experience of our true being. 'I, the soul, the point, am here and the Supreme Soul, also a point of light, is up there'. However, love and remembrance bring such closeness that there is no feeling of distance or separation.

To achieve remembrance that empowers, we need to plug in every day to the Supreme Source in silence, in a way that is beyond ritual or sound. It is a personal connection, which requires no audience and no rules, only an honest heart. When a person is well-intentioned, the plug of love fits into the socket and the self receives whatever it needs, whatever is useful for it to create and sustain a life of quality.

> *In order to remember to create a quality life, ask the self 'What is my highest ideal?'*

Know it, understand it, follow it, be it, no matter what happens. Remember: I achieve what I believe.

11

EIGHT PRINCIPLES OF SPIRITUAL LIVING

THERE IS SOMETIMES the misconception that meditation keeps us in the clouds beyond reality. Frequently, people think it is an escape. However, for those who meditate appropriately, meditation (that is, the art of listening, reflecting and concentrating) brings us to a point where we are empowered and, therefore, able to face life positively and realistically.

Let us take a look at the principles of spiritual living. There are eight fundamental principles that, together with our own reflection and silence, help us practically in daily life.

Principle 1: Observe and not Absorb

To observe means we take a new mental position in whatever situation, or with whatever relationship, we find ourselves. Observation is a silent skill – a skill we need to learn if we are to assess clearly what positive changes are needed in a particular situation, or in relation to a person. To be a detached observer means to keep the mind clear and free and, therefore, open to new perspectives as we learn to listen and tune into the reality of the other.

> *Being able to observe enables us to be creative, productive and effective because we have made space for true and better understanding.*

If we fail to learn this art of observing, we are likely to react and absorb ourselves in the negativity of the person, or event. We get lost in the quicksand of 'What's wrong?' which prevents us from putting things right. As we absorb and fill ourselves with negative emotion, we become heavy and remain helplessly rooted to the ground. The gravity of overload does not allow us to rise above a situation and to perceive the reality of what is happening. As a result, we lose perspective and overreact.

If we wish to understand how the mental position of observation gives us the power of perspective, we can look at the example of the bird and the ant. The ant, extremely busy, running here and there, scrambling over everything in its rush to find and collect food, will see only what is in front of its nose. The bird, on the other hand, leaves the earth and, as it flies higher and higher, starts to see the bigger picture, compared to when it was on the ground, or on the branch of a tree. Seeing the whole picture, it has a completely different perspective. It is only then that it can truly see where to go and what to do.

When we lose perspective, we get too involved in the details, missing the 'obvious', and cannot imagine, or think of other realities.

Principle 2: To be Aware but not Judgemental

On the path of Raja Yoga meditation there is a saying, "See, but don't see! Hear, but don't hear!" which means to remain aware of all realities, including the negative, but not to focus on them. We get caught up in the negative because we react and the reactions manifest themselves as judgements, accusations, criticism, or labelling. We do all this when we feel threatened by what we are unfamiliar with, when we are moved out of our comfort zones. As soon as we judge or criticise, we put everything into convenient boxes and, just as convenience foods are not always so healthy, such mental and attitudinal conveniences are a great danger, because we mentally seal the fate of the person or situation: they are like this and so must be treated accordingly. Unfortunately, this is often done in an unconscious way, which is why Raja Yoga meditation is used to bring such attitudes and behaviours to the surface, conscious awareness.

When our vision and attitude remain judgemental or critical, they do so because there is no input of positivity from the self to encourage or allow a positive change.

> *There cannot be a positive output when there is a negative input.*

We frequently work in this way, wanting others to be better in some way, but, instead of helping them, or having faith in them and seeing their good qualities, we hinder them by concentrating on their past, their weaknesses and their mistakes. Our focus is completely negative, but still we expect them to change for the better!

When our awareness is more detached, rather than focusing on what is wrong, we look at how we can put something right by contributing a positive feeling, or attitude. This anonymous and benevolent contribution is a generous act, which offers a solution, instead of the usual complaints proffered by critical and judgemental people.

A spiritually aware person offers remedies and does not indulge in self-righteous complaints.

Maturity means to be fully aware and, to the extent one is aware, to keep silent. Many things work themselves out when our own input is consistently kind and honestly motivated.

Principle 3: Focus and Flow

If we look at the sun and the earth, we appreciate a basic and fundamental law of function, which we as human beings can learn from, that is of paramount help in the right movement of life. By means of light, the sun gives life to the earth; in addition, the sun is fixed in its position to enable the earth and all the other planets of our solar system to continue in their rhythmic, harmonious orbit. Otherwise, there would be chaos, upheaval and great damage. The earth, on the other hand, constantly moves in repetitive cycles around the sun. This movement allows for change and expression, which have a beginning, middle and end. In other words, the phenomenon of time is created as a direct result of the earth's balanced and harmonious cyclic rhythms. Both the fixed position of the sun and the movement of the earth are necessary for life. The earth has all the potential for life but, without light from a fixed source, there would be no life. In the same way, the sun has the power to give life, but if the moving earth did not hold the potential, even with light, there would be no manifestation of life.

In certain situations and moments we need focus, that is, a concentration of thought, will and understanding. These three need to be together in one focused point if we are to reach depth and newness. However, if we become over-focused, then rigidity and pressure gradually set in. This subsequently leads to an imbalance that makes us lose creativity and openness to new vision. Once we have learnt to focus, then it will require less effort and, eventually, the flow will become natural.

> *In focus, we find vision, inspiration and understanding, and in the flow, we find expression, experimentation and experience.*

It is important not to over-flow, otherwise we get lost in a flood of over-thinking, over-speaking and overdoing. In such a state, there is no direction to guide the expression and things become vague and fragile. At such a point, we need to recognise that it is time for focus again.

According to necessity, a human being needs to move between focus and flow and it is only through the *ability to discern* that we can know when and how to do this. Everything has its time. We are eternal beings working in time, so we need to know the balance between the focus of eternity - where we find truth and purpose - and the flow of time - where we find expression and experience.

Principle 4: Stepping In and Stepping Out

For any activity, or relationship to remain harmonious and successful, we must know how far to step in and how far to step out. It is like a gardener who sows seeds at the right time, steps in to plant and water them and then steps out of the picture to allow nature to carry on with her work. However, from time to time, he steps in again to see if there is enough water, if any insects are attacking the plants, if any food is needed. His role is to find the appropriate space for the potential beauty and uniqueness of the seeds to emerge; he does not create the flowers but facilitates their expression.

The gardener does not step in too much; that would be called interference. After planting the seeds, he does not demand an immediate result; he does not dig them up next day to see if they have sprouted. He plays his role, fulfils his duty, but lets go because he understands the blooming of the flowers is not dependent on him. Nor does he let go too much. If he did, then the plants would die from lack of care, or the insects and weeds would overpower them. He does not let go so much that he isolates himself from the process. Instead, by knowing when to step in and when to step out, he creates a respectful partnership with nature.

In the same way, we have the duty, or rather the honour, of planting positive seeds of good intention, respect and tolerance, at the same time allowing others and the forces of the universe to be given the space to work and respond according to their time and inclination.

Very often we plant those seeds but want an immediate result: "I have shown so much patience, but he doesn't change." or "How much longer do I have to be tolerant? I feel suppressed." We become attached to what we do, so there is no space for things to happen in their own appropriate time. Sometimes we have the wrong type of mercy, or we want to take control, thinking we know better, so we step into people's lives too much. This interference and lack of free space provokes antagonism, resentment and conflict with others.

At other times, we get fed up with others; our tolerance and empathy is completely reduced and we say, "I've had enough", or "I have got to do my own thing" and so we step out, but in a selfish way, that is, we isolate ourselves from others, or situations. We justify, or disguise, this rejection and dislike with such phrases as, "I need my own space" or "Let them stand on their own feet." In actual fact, we can't be bothered any more; we have stepped too far out of the picture because we have not cultivated the patient understanding which allows the good and positive to germinate and grow in its own time.

It is an art to know when to step back and when to step forward, but a very necessary one if well-being is to be achieved.

Principle 5 : Complementarity

Harmony, well-being and the fulfilment of individual purpose are only possible when our consciousness is inclusive, rather than exclusive, that is, a consciousness that is universal in the sense that we can recognise and appreciate the purpose and necessity of all things in life and, therefore, give them the space to express their innate right to be.

When people, either on an individual or collective level, become exclusive, that is, when the foundation of their identity is based on prerogative and privilege, then harmony, peace and certainly love are lost both in the individual and in society. Individuals, societies, nations, religions and politics become exclusive when they are attributed a particular speciality, talent, or position. While it is healthy and necessary to value *who* you are, it becomes most unhealthy and violent to become attached to your special qualities, making others feel inferior because they do not possess those same qualities. The reason for conflict, on any level, is nearly always this sense of right to dominate or suppress others because we feel we are better in one way or another.

Unfortunately, in modern society, both East and West, the idea of outdoing others in order to prove the value of the person, or idea, has taken precedence over the innate principle of life, which is complementarity.

> *When we learn to complement rather than compete, there will be peace and, above all, self-respect.*

Self-respect means to recognise myself as I am and thus fulfil my purpose without injury to, or comparison with, others. We all have a place within this beautiful tapestry of life; let us know it, enjoy it, express it as our right, but never overdo it because we feel our role or position is 'more advanced', or 'better' than others. Sometimes, when there is a sense of personal or collective inadequacy, there is the need to be recognised, which creates attachment to privilege and prerogative. When a sense of identity is based on these, it creates exclusivity.

Nature works on the principle of complementarity. This can be seen with the seasons, day and night, the continual cyclical process of birth, growth, maturity, decay, death and rebirth. Even our bodies work on this principle. Look at the face! Each face has two eyes, one nose, one mouth, two ears, all in the right position and functioning in an appropriate way. Which of these is more important? Would you say the eyes are more important, so you would prefer to have three eyes and no nose? Or would you say the nose is more important, so you would prefer to have three noses and no ears? We cannot think like this because it is absurd and illogical. Each feature has equal value and when we recognise the equal value of all things, then we stop being illogical–comparing, competing, feeling superior or inferior, or striving to be what we are not. In a society that functions, can everyone be a doctor, a builder or a baker? Everyone has different talents and positions because different tasks have to be fulfilled if the whole society is to run well.

If we examine life carefully, we realise that the recognition of this principle of complementarity is the basis of creating a peaceful and happy coexistence, because the vision and attitude of equality respects and honours the differences.

Principle 6: The Individual and the Collective

There are two faces to the one coin; a person who wishes to live fully as a human being needs to understand that the existence of one's unique individuality has to be acknowledged, as well as the existence of the collective. One cannot exist without the other, although many people have gone to the extremes of both with very damaging results. Those systems which develop the collective aspect at the expense of the individual become rigid, autocratic, cruel and uncreative, often imposing a sterile uniformity on human thought and action in the belief that this is the way to maintain harmony and order. Those systems (whether social, religious, or political) that develop individualism above everything else, create narcissism and self-indulgence, resulting in a personal sense of isolation. This alienation is often the result of not developing the values of tolerance and acceptance, which are such a necessary part of human coexistence.

Individuals who are developing spiritually feel a personal sense of value. They clearly recognise their uniqueness without any false humility and have the feeling that there is the freedom to be whatever they choose to be.

Simultaneously, their sense of personal independence allows them to come close to others and work with them. They do not have selfish independence. They get close to others because they have found fulfilment in their own self.

> *People who have truly discovered the value of the self will never confine themselves to, or exaggerate their worth with, an illusory identity based on labels and external achievements.*

Someone who has truly found the value of the self above and beyond labels, name, fame and approval, can effectively cooperate within the collective and interact appropriately. Such people not only feel themselves to be a part of the whole but, even more significantly, the collective feels them to be a part of the whole.

In nature, when birds have to fly to a warmer climate in winter, they flock together and start their journey as a collective. The success of the journey depends on the collective: if an individual bird does not join the group, it cannot reach the destination on its own. Birds fly in a particular formation, with an appropriate space between them as they fly. If they fly too close to each other, their wings get entangled, they lose their balance and fall. If they remain too far from each other, the formation cannot be created properly, and they are not able to ride the currents of air, which help to propel them in their flight. Furthermore, the leader of the formation does not remain the leader throughout the whole flight, but moves back and allows another to take its place. This repositioning continues throughout the flight until the destination is reached, allowing individual birds to contribute to the success of the journey.

> *The reality of life is that we are individuals within a collective whole.*

If the collective respects the space of the individual, then it functions to serve the individual's aspirations and differences. Otherwise, if the collective does not respect that space, it becomes repressive. In short, the individual needs to respect the collective and not go to the extremes of personal rights, and the collective must respect the individual and not go to the extremes in its use of systems.

Principle Seven: Faith

What we believe comes true. What we believe is the reflection of our deepest held ideas and thoughts, which, in one way or another, are present at every moment of our lives. It has been said that faith can move mountains.

The highest mountains are our negative thoughts, feelings and ideas, which hinder our capacity to rise beyond our limits.

Faith is the energy of understanding that enables us to realise anything is possible even if it is not visible in front of our eyes, but, more especially, even if it is not visible in front of our reason.

The success that comes from faith is closely linked with 'letting go'. It is only when we let go of what we are used to, or what we have learnt to depend on, that new perceptions and new possibilities are given to us.

Our life is like that of a pole vaulter. We have used many tools in our life, which at their time were valuable and necessary but now have to be discarded because other items are necessary. The same applies to people who wish for a deeper spiritual experience when they use knowledge. Knowledge is very necessary and without it we cannot rise to the heights we wish but, equally, at one point, we have to let go of the support of knowledge and jump. To jump over the barrier of habit, custom and comfort is not simply a matter of knowledge, but also to dare the self to enter another dimension of consciousness. To be willing to experiment requires faith and cannot be done if we remain within our comfort zones.

With faith, it is not necessary to analyse and know everything in detail before doing something.

All that is needed are a few basic facts and then we can take action. When we drive a car, do we insist on knowing how the engine works in detail before driving it? Do we know the mechanical details of an elevator before we use it? Most people are only aware of the basic functions and this is all they need to carry out the action. However, they do have the faith that the car has been correctly constructed to do its job safely and that by pressing a few buttons the elevator will take them to wherever it is they want to go. In the modern world, there is a tendency to over-think, to want to control and direct every outcome, but such a life lacks spontaneity and simplicity.

Although we do need a framework, it must be flexible enough to allow space for the unexpected, the unpredictable and the great surprise. Such a space is the window through which the light of innovation can enter. When life is over-planned, we become cemented in, unable to grow, or flow, into new horizons. Faith allows us to realise that optimum results can happen without always having to structure or plan. Such faith is the basis for new vision and allows us to reach beyond our limits; because we believe we are more than meets the eye.

Such faith is the inspirational energy of every pioneer in whatever field.

Principle 8: Relationship with the Unconditional Source

There is one point of being in the universe who is not conditioned by any need, want or desire. Since He does not want anything, everything belongs to Him, but not in the sense of owning and controlling. Rather, all things naturally gravitate to the Unconditional Source simply because pure love is given freely to all who come close. They feel that He selflessly serves, sharing all that He is, all that He has. Like a radiant Magnet beyond the limits of time and matter, beyond give and take and beyond measurement and calculation, the Source attracts all because nothing is desired and all is given.

The love of the Unconditional Source is like spiritual sunlight. It is selfless, complete in itself: it always adds and never subtracts. What is unconditional is always cherished to the point of worship, which is probably why God and real saints are venerated in all parts of the world. Spiritual light from the Source reveals to us our forgotten realities, our hidden potential and our original goodness. It reveals our true selves. Then, if we wish, we can nourish and develop that awareness, but only to the extent that we maintain an open channel of communication. Otherwise, the current either short circuits, cuts, blocks, or discharges in other directions and, after a while, there is a blackout! Humanity, at the moment, is in the blackout phase.

> *Meditation is the mental exercise to link ourselves to that Unconditional Source. As we make that link, purification takes place, liberating the mind from the limits of "I", "my", the past, resentments and pettiness.*

During meditation the mind lets go of the threads of the limited. Like a bird, the mind flies up and connects to God. This connection is not difficult when the mind is truly in love with knowing the truth and not just trying to demand, cajole, or beg God for something for selfish reasons. When there is just a desire for connection, the soul feels a magnetic pull that enables it to fly beyond all impossible barriers such as "I can't", "How?" and "No time!". Connection fills the soul with a spiritual strength that keeps it constantly positive, uninfluenced by any external negativity.

Meditation helps us to gain this inner spiritual strength, especially when we use it in our everyday life. To maintain such strength, we require a daily connection and recharge every morning. In silence, the human being finds a personal and benevolent friendship with God, who not only listens and helps but, most of all, is just there. Human beings have completely lost the simple enjoyment of His presence; they feel they have to ask for something, say something, or chant something. It is enough just to be still in the silence of that spiritual meeting and be content.

12

BALANCE AND HARMONY

HARMONY WITHIN THE self and with others is based on the accuracy of three aspects of remembrance: the ability to *disconnect, connect and reconnect.*

> *When I disconnect my thoughts from outside influences, stepping back from actions and words, then I can go into silence and connect with the self.*

To plug into the self, I use the thought: Om Shanti. This thought is the current that activates my eternal resource of peace and the qualities that emanate from this peace. The first step in meditation is always to connect with the self: what we call the inward step.

The next step in meditation is vertical, where, within one second, my concentrated thought connects my mind with the Supreme Source of Peace.

Silence and love give the mind wings to break the pull of gravity and to fly and unite with the One, who is the purist point of energy in the universe. This vertical connection from the point of the self, the soul, to the point of the universe, the Supreme Soul, gives the mind fresh new energy. This fresh energy is divine spiritual power and cannot be found in, or taken from, a human being. Therefore, if I wish to recharge myself, to rediscover and restore the original balance and harmony within myself, the second movement made by my mind must be vertical.

Today, when human beings seek love, meaning and purpose, they first connect horizontally rather than vertically. This leads to a greater loss of energy and eventually dissatisfaction and emptiness. The vertical connection liberates the self from becoming dependent on someone else and from having too many expectations.

After the vertical connection, there can then be the horizontal connection with others, that is, with the outside or external.

The horizontal movement can be called 'reconnection'. When we have taken the other two steps (first inwards and then upwards), we reconnect with others on the basis of openness and sharing, rather than selfishness and need. At this point, there is a real relationship that is respectful and balanced, rather than a relationship of wanting, taking, or exploiting. We have come to understand that when we are well with ourselves, we will be well with others.

> *All three points of connection are necessary for good emotional and spiritual health.*

If I am only connected inwards, there is a great danger of arrogance and being lost in only myself. If I am only connected to the Supreme Source with little reference to myself, or others, there is the danger of becoming rigid, fanatical and unrealistic. If I am over-focused on others, then a dependence is created, which results in conflict and disappointment. The latter is an inevitable result of over-focusing on relationships with others, thinking I will receive my happiness and sense of purpose from them.

> *When I do reconnect with the outside world, it can only be done effectively from the vantage point of connection with the self and with One.*

This three-point connection can be depicted in the form of a triangle with the self as a point, then the vertical movement upward to the Supreme Point:

Then the horizontal connection to others:

Others need to have their own independent and personal connection with the Supreme Point to revitalise and renew their own consciousness. In this way, the triangle of harmonious energy becomes complete:

All three points need to be equidistant – not too much one way or the other. The 'equidistant triangle' in ancient mathematics was the symbol of harmony. Harmony, peace, order and balance is what is natural in human life and if we wish to return to that condition, we need to realise the importance of equidistant relationships. It requires constant attention to keep the three in balance and in working order. Otherwise, when we get over-focused on any one of the three, we become inflexible. This inflexibility causes us to go out of balance and the result is disharmony and disunity, which can also be called 'violence', an unnatural condition, or even hell when it reaches an extreme point.

In order to maintain a balance between the three, I need silence: times of introspection when I can check the flow of my relationships. This checking mechanism protects, sustains and develops the qualities of these three points.

13

MOTIVATION

MEDITATION, IN THE form of reflection and examination, helps me to create and maintain my motivation. For newness and clarity of perception, ideals and aims, we need to relax our grip on old habits, on old ways of thinking and seeing and thus create a space for something new and inspirational.

> *Motivation is an inner positive energy, a combination of enthusiasm and clear perception that enables us to accomplish a task.*

Motivation keeps us determined and on course, otherwise it is so easy to be distracted by problems, novelties and laziness. What does motivation do? It moves us from one reality to another, from where I am to where I wish to be. Motivation is sustained when a sense of purpose, identity and contribution is being fulfilled.

When we want to reactivate our motivation we need to examine the following:

> What do I want?
> What do I wish for?
> What do I value?
> What do I need?
> What do I enjoy?
> What do I understand? and, especially,
> What do I love?

When we sit down and reflect on the answers to these questions, they become the basis for activating new insights and tasks and for reactivating those insights and tasks, which I have forgotten to pay proper attention to and have not developed properly. Throughout life it is necessary, from time to time, to stand back, become silent and redefine, re-evaluate, and experiment, over and over again, with what we know, or what we think we know. It is a simple exercise, which, if done sincerely, stimulates newness in our thoughts and in our motivational pattern.

Therefore, to change, or widen, my pattern I need to

> redefine
> re-examine
> reorientate
> relearn

Then newness, creativity and quality are generated.

Successful motivation depends on having a clear aim. How much do I believe in my aim? Faith in my aim determines the quality of effort and willingness to meet challenges. There will be successful renewal of motivation when I realise that there is always the opportunity to exercise the power of choice.

Another question which helps us in sustaining motivation is, "What is really most important to me: product or process?" Process entails growth, development and learning: a cultivation of the awareness and resources of the self and others. To be product-orientated tends to over-focus on result with not enough care or attention to the underlying processes needed to arrive at that result. The quick-fix method, the 'success in 7 days' formula, does not really work, at least not permanently. If we look at nature, we see that her beauty and her strength are the combined result of time and process. For example, a huge oak tree, the roses in the garden, the changing of the seasons do not happen instantly. There is always space and time given for particular processes to function.

> *For a process to happen effectively, I need to prioritise, that is, to make the best use of my time, energy and resources.*

To prioritise, I also need to recognise and refuse clever excuses (for example, 'there is no time') and create a timetable that is realistic and functional. As I prioritise my values, then the type of motivation I have becomes clearer. Is my motivation materialistic or spiritual? The results of one and the other are very different.

Materialistic motivation is based on ambition, competition and a desire for position. Often we believe we cannot succeed without these and so think and act on the basis of these values. Often the results include conflict, fear, attachment, jealousy, possessiveness and over-identification of the self with a role, a position, which makes us feel threatened by anyone who is more talented or more praised. For example, when motivation is materialistic, there is always the fear of loss that, in turn, creates uneasiness, stress and worry.

Spiritual motivation is based on enthusiasm for a task, rather than blind ambition, co-operation with the uniqueness of others, rather than being in competition with those differences. Finally, the feeling to serve through whatever talent, position, or role I have: to serve a need rather than exploit a need is quality service.

> *The results of spiritual motivation are respect, harmony, individual and collective well-being, a sense of purpose and the feeling of a deep fulfilment in one's being.*

Spiritual motives such as cooperation, sharing, caring, integrity and respect create quality in the aim, the task and the methodology used. Meditation, in the form of reflection, always helps me to re-examine and redefine my aims, my processes and the reasons why I am doing what I am doing.

14

COMMUNICATION

A GREAT DEAL of our communication is non-verbal and we rarely realise the impact that it has on others. Our tone of voice, our body language (particularly our eyes and face), our attitudes and our feelings, are constantly in communication with others, expressing anger, fear, love, trust, rejection – in fact, all our emotions. We cannot hide what we mean; we may do so for a while, but eventually the truth emerges.

> *In order to communicate clearly, the primary step is silence, that is, the ability to listen.*

In addition to listening, communication is also about sharing, understanding and enjoying what the other has to offer. Genuine communication heals and nurtures.

Communication is not just with others, but also with the self, with God and even nature. Being still, focused and open enables us to tune in to others so that we can respond in an appropriate and meaningful way, not simply in a mechanical way.

What are the blocks to positive communication? When we communicate, do we reflect, or deflect what we mean? Is what we communicate clear, or confusing to others?

Here are some common reasons for blocks to communication:

*   A plethora of thoughts, words and actions *overload,* results in us being unable to think clearly. We lose the essence of what is trying to be conveyed

*   *Being* lost in our own emotions or ideas. In such a state we do not listen attentively to others

*   *Remembering the past in a negative way.* This does not allow us to tune in properly to our present and future. When we do not communicate properly with the needs of the present time, we loose opportunities

*   *Lack of sincerity.* When our thoughts and feelings are honest and respectful, then the hearts of others will

open to us. A positive highway of trust is built and communication flows positively

- *Creating* negative perceptions and feelings about others i.e. how we visualise or label them. Such feelings, no matter how well hidden, are eventually always communicated to others on a subtle, non-verbal level, and create an atmosphere of tension and unease

- *Not letting go of negative perceptions and feelings.* The only method to renew our relationship with others is to let go of negativity on a daily basis, to prevent it from building up. Far too often, the build-up happens without us even noticing it and, we wonder why positive feedback is not forthcoming

- *Lack of silence.* To go deep into the self and put our thoughts and feelings into the quarantine of silence enables them to become positive. The quarantine of silent relaxation defuses anger and the blame and complaints that often go with it

What are the ways to improve communication?

- *Listen with both ears.* I should be an active listener by tuning in fully and being present fully with the person and with the moment. If I am not, I listen through one ear and let it out of the other, or I only half listen, which inevitably creates misunderstandings

- *Understand where the other person is coming from.* Do not just assume, imagine or judge; when we do this, our critical vision inhibits others from expressing what they wish to say. Then, because of wrong or half-right assumptions, others are not given the possibility to move, or express, outside our imposed frame of reference. To give others a true chance to express themselves, we must not place our own frames around them.

- *Think before speaking.* This is not something new, but however often we hear it, we forget to apply it. To think before speaking means to show consideration to the other and then we say the right thing, at the right time, in the right way.

- *Say what we mean, always.* When we speak with courage and a calm self-confidence without force, then communication is honest, open, clear and trusted. Courage doesn't mean to say what we think others want to hear. If we lack courage because of the need for approval and acceptance, or because of a lack of confidence, then communication and the consequent relationship remains superficial and artificial. No one feels satisfied with this situation.

- *Learn the language of silence.* It is the basis of right intention, positive feelings and clear attitudes. In this language, there is only one grammar: honesty and kindness. Honesty creates clarity and kindness creates respectfulness.

When we take time to reflect on our level of communication with everyone we meet, the realisations we have in silence will be manifested in the higher quality and ease of interaction that we will find in all relations: be it with the self, with others or with the Supreme Source of Light.

15

OVERCOMING FEAR

FEAR COMES DAILY and often in our lives in the form of stress, worry, anxiety and in a variety of other wasteful and negative forms. For example, stress is one of the biggest diseases of the 21st century. Originally the word 'stress' was only used for the pressure, or tension, exerted on a machine: engineers build in a calculation for stress to ensure that the machine functions correctly. Gradually, however, the term has become more and more popular to describe the state of human beings.

When we try to describe stress, a whole chain of words such as 'push', 'pull', 'pressure', 'more', or 'deadlines' comes to mind. To have to produce, to do more and more and to be better and better at it, creates a lot of tension, which comes from the fear of not being able to achieve the result on time.

The materialistic values of getting, having, accumulating and outdoing others in the form of ambition, competition and position produce a lot of stress.

When we are stressed, we are certainly overloaded. We think and speak too much and we overreact, all of which affect both body and mind negatively. The worst thing is that this becomes a habit, which is often uncontrolled, and so the simple remedy of stopping and relaxing, is not considered as a remedy. Some even regard it as a useless waste of time.

However, before we explore how to overcome fears generally, let us look at some of the types of fear human beings suffer from:

- *The unknown* - for example, death or a new situation

- *Loneliness* - sometimes people fear loneliness to the extent that they cannot bear their own company, preferring to lose themselves in superficial relationships and activities

- *The future* - as the crises of the world increase, whether political, economic, environmental or social, this creates, or adds to, personal and collective fear of the future

- *Illness* - sometimes because of fear of disease, people make their sickness worse than it is, or live in dread of getting something horrible

- *Other people* - usually this is the greatest fear of all: fear of others' anger, rejection, judgement and violence

- *Failure* - some people avoid doing something, or choose not to act, because their fear of failure paralyses initiative and confidence

- *Authority* - this can be fear of a parent, of a director, even of God. Because authority has often been misused, or misrepresented, in order to control and suppress people, it is a normal consequence that fear, in the form of suspicion and mistrust, has become such a negative force, both personally and collectively, in society.

There are many reasons for these types of fear, but the main ones include:

- *Past experiences*, which brought disappointment, insecurity, or wariness

- *Lack of faith* in one's self and in others

- *The need for approval,* to belong, or to be accepted

- *The habit of seeing things negatively*

One of the greatest products of fear is doubt.

When a person is lost in doubt, he cannot believe in the solutions and answers given, not even to the point of experimenting with them or trying to see if they could work. Doubt in an extreme form creates such uncertainty and insecurity that a person suffers from mental, and even emotional, paralysis. There is either a freeze up, or panic, where no initiative for being positive is possible. The mind is plagued by questions of 'How?', 'When?', 'Why?, or 'What?'. Questions are not posed to really find answers but to prolong hesitation, or keep the self on the defensive, or in a state of non-commitment, not really listening or wanting to know. To enquire is a different thing from doubt; when there is enquiry, there are constructive questions, an openness to learn and a willingness to experiment.

When there is any type of fear, which may be expressed through doubt, jealousy, secrecy or competitiveness, there is neither openness nor willingness. At the core of it all, there is the fear of loss, either of a person, position, possession or one's image.   All fears, whether subtle or gross, result in dependence, expectation and, ultimately, conflict, either with one's own self or with others.

How can we overcome fear?

Before participating or reacting, we often need to relax, become calm and observe so that our contribution is appropriate and positive.

Learn to observe:

How do I see myself?

     As valuable?

     With the right to be?

     Can I face myself?

     Do I like, accept and respect myself?

How do I see others?

     Friends?

     Enemies?

     Teachers?

     Supports?

     Extensions to me?

     Valuable?

How do I see life? Primarily as:
> Joy or pain?
> Gift or curse?
> Game or battle?
> Learning or losing?

If we go through these questions quietly and slowly and give ourself time to think about them, the answers will make us aware of whether we are building walls, or bridges, in our life. Are there only bridges, or only walls, or both? More bridges, or more walls? The negative answer is a wall; the positive answer is a bridge.

Here are some ways to build more bridges and fewer walls:

Trust - Learn to trust because trusting the self, others and life opens unforeseen possibilities. Do not worry too much if you are cheated, if the other is not true, if, if, if - leave the 'ifs', and do. As is said, 'nothing ventured, nothing gained'.

Faith - Jump over barriers; do not make them into excuses. If we do not accept challenges, our life is one of a 'boring safety' whose foundation is fear of newness or change. It may appear safe and comfortable but it is an illusory security, which can break at any time, in any way.

Acceptance - Mistakes, setbacks, failures, disappointments are part of the growing and knowing process and should not be condemned or feared. Every human being has gone through it, is going through it and will continue to do so.

Remaining Light - All things have their meaning and, if not now, eventually, we will understand that meaning. It is healthy for mind and body not to carry the burden of exaggeration and lack of perspective.

Life is a Game - Know the rules and play it well. A good player is aware, then easy, tolerant and flexible, does not get stuck on a scene, a rule, or any other player for too long, gives due respect and attention but keeps moving. A good player plays his own part and does not try to play the part of others.

Self-respect - Let us acknowledge our spiritual reality as a human being with quality resources inside that need to be always opened up and used. We do not need to accept false supports from the outside, such as name, fame and praise. We are what we are because of what is inside us. Our reference point is that which is eternal and valuable inside; then there cannot be the fear of being damaged.

Silence and Positive Outlook - When we realise the importance of being silent and still from time to time, then our positivity towards self and life is re-examined and renewed. Otherwise, the speed and immensity of negative forces, whether from the self, or from others, will certainly make us fearful.

Let us remove ourselves from the pressures of life and learn to break the chains of fear that bind us and prevent us from making spiritual progress.

16

NEXT STEPS

EACH DAY IS a chance to learn, to heal and to see the inherent goodness of others. When we forget these things we become polluted by stress and animosity. How to remember when there seems to be so much to get done, and so much negativity to face? The theory is inspiring, but in practice how can it all be achieved?

We nurture the soul by going into the depths of silence and learning to love and appreciate the self. Giving time to do this will bring about a change in how we go about doing things, and this will start to show itself in improved relationships and in quality of life. By adopting a systematic and practical approach, we can assist the changes we wish to bring about in our life, otherwise old patterns of behaviour and the influences of the world will undermine our resolve and efforts, like the tide washing away a sandcastle.

Here are some practical reminders and steps we can take to aid our spiritual growth and transformation.

1. *Create a space for silence*
Creating a space for inner silence is important and we can also create a corner area or a room used only for this purpose. In that place there is the opportunity, for instance, each morning to prepare for the coming day and, in the evening, to unburden the mind of any wasteful thoughts and feelings that have accumulated.

2, *Daily practice*
Having the inner discipline to practise meditation by one's self is necessary because, in reality, we have to be self reliant as only we can step into our mind and bring it long-term benefit. The mind needs to relax and to refresh itself if a person is to feel positive and strong to live each day peacefully and effectively. When this is recognized, time for inner silence every day becomes a personal priority.

Start each day with positive silence. Before work, breakfast, or doing anything, let us step inside the self for a little while.

In this space of introversion, we can connect with our original spiritual qualities, charging up our internal battery with positive thoughts for the day ahead.

At the end of the day, we can discard any remaining thoughts of past actions – after all *'past is past'* - and send out good wishes where they are needed.

Having connected with the best in the self, it helps us to live more consciously, so that we are able to deal with everything more effectively.

The daily practice of morning preparation and evening clearing, keeps the mind healthy. A healthy mind is light and focused, not distracted, or burdened easily.

3. Use 'traffic control'

To remember our original peaceful state during certain moments of the day creates a space for us to recharge and to be released from accumulated negativities, which have influenced our mind without our realizing it.

'Traffic control', as mentioned previously, is a method to check and control the flow and type of thoughts that we create. Are our thoughts wasteful or are they useful, necessary, positive, and peaceful? By stopping for a minute on the hour, every hour, we can step inside, apply a brake to the flow of thoughts and instead focus on the experience *I am a peaceful being.* This practice has an immediate cooling effect on the mind, and if done regularly, has a very positive impact on our daily lives.

4. Attend a meditation centre

The starting point is knowledge, or understanding. It is not possible to begin this journey without some kind of route map. There are centres of Raja Yoga meditation throughout the world that provide these maps and help a person begin his, or her, practice of meditation. Information is shared on how the mind functions, the power of positivity, spiritual values and the art of effective concentration. All of these maps help us to know ourselves better and, when translated into our personal daily life, give us strength in the form of self-respect and happiness.

A Raja Yoga meditation centre is a spiritual school, where we can learn the original arts of true living; it is a spiritual clinic, where we receive the understanding of how to apply the healing medicines of peace, trust and respect in our relationships; it is a spiritual family, where we realize that each member has a uniqueness and goodness that needs to be appreciated and genuinely accepted, and where we pay attention to avoiding the trap of focusing on weaknesses and the roles of others.

5. *Meditate with others*

Another great help in maintaining a stable grounding on the path of meditation, is collective practice. Through personal practice, I keep my sense of responsibility intact and remain independent. However, without losing these, I can also integrate with others, valuing and learning from their experiences and perceptions - the group dynamic brings us to another level of experience, a space of mutual experience and learning. We learn from everyone, everywhere, all the time; it depends on our willingness to accept certain realities. For example, our attitude towards time is more responsible and positive when we are more reflective about how we engage in every moment.

Often we live too much in the past, or future, and so do not realize that the present is the bridge to moving away from the negativity of the past and to creating a confident future. We do not cross this bridge because we live by, or are too influenced by, the other two time zones.

Remember that NOW is the opportunity where newness on any level can be created.

6. Develop a spiritual lifestyle

The daily practice of meditation will be aided if we change those aspects of our life that affect, or undermine, our ability to control the mind and live in a state of peace. For example, taking mind-altering substances like alcohol and drugs, watching violent films or following pursuits that re-enforce old patterns of behaviour that take us away from our true self.

Many changes happen easily and naturally as we begin to experience the benefits of meditation. Our desires for material objects beyond those that are necessary for daily living fall away as we seek to live a simpler, quieter life. We gain a deeper respect for nature and loose the desire to eat animal flesh, and we become more selective about the company we keep and the things we talk about, realizing that everything we say and do has an impact on the world around us.

As our self esteem and confidence subsequently grow, we feel ourselves drawn to help others, to share the benefits we have learned from our own inner journey. Life becomes filled with greater meaning and purpose and we want to do our best for ourselves, for our families and for our communities.

7. Get Started!

The main part of any journey is to start. Sometimes we hesitate, sometimes we make excuses, but we must not give in to these thoughts. When we accept the challenge to try, the journey begins. When we agree to take the first steps, success is there waiting for us. Faith in ourselves brings optimism to what we do. Optimism and faith open the *Horizon of Possibility*, an inner knowing of what good could be there which, as yet, I cannot see, or even imagine.

It is said, 'Nothing ventured, nothing gained.' So why not venture? Why not gain?

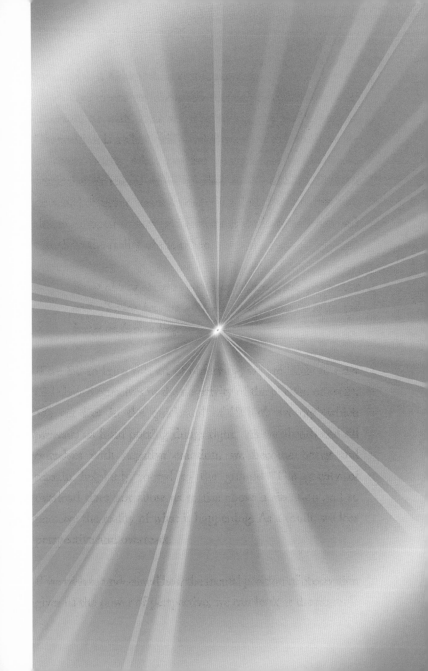

Other books to feed the soul

If you have enjoyed reading this book on Raja Yoga meditation as taught by the Brahma Kumaris World Spiritual University, you might like to read the following books to enhance your meditation practice and deepen your spiritual understanding.

All the above books and a variety of meditation commentaries and meditation music are available from
www.bkpublications.com

About the Brahma Kumaris
World Spiritual University

The Brahma Kumaris World Spiritual University is an international organisation working at all levels of society for positive change. Established in 1937, the University now has over 8,000 centres in more than 90 countries. It actively participates in a wide range of educational programmes in areas such as youth, women, men, environment, peace, values, social development, education, health and human rights.

In 1996, the University's Academy for a Better World was opened in Mount Abu, India. The Academy offers individuals from all walks of life opportunities for life-long innovative learning. Residential programmes are centred on human, moral and spiritual values and principles. The University also supports the Global Hospital and Research Centre in Mount. Abu , India.

Local centres around the world provide courses and lectures in meditation and positive values, supporting individuals in recognising their own inherent qualities and abilities, and making the most of their lives.

All courses and activities are offered free of charge.

International Headquarters
Po Box No 2, Mount Abu 307501,
Rajasthan, India.
Tel: (+91) 2974-38261 to 68
Fax: (+91) 2974-38952
E-mail: abu@bkindia.com

International Co-Ordinating Office &
Regional Office For Europe And The Middle East
Global Co-operation House,
65-69 Pound Lane, London, NW10 2HH, UK
Tel: (+44) 208 727 3350
Fax: (+44) 208 727 3351
E-mail: london@bkwsu.com

REGIONAL OFFICES

Africa
Global Museum for a Better World,
Maua Close, off Parklands Road, Westlands,
PO Box 123, Sarit Centre, Nairobi, Kenya
Tel: (+254) 20-374 3572
Fax: (+254) 20-374 3885
E-mail: bkwsugm@holidaybazaar.com

Australia And South East Asia
78 Alt Street, Ashfield, Sydney, NSW 2131, Australia
Tel: (+61) 2 9716 7066
Fax: (+61) 2 9716 7795
E-mail: indra@brahmakumaris.com.au

The Americas And The Caribbean
Global Harmony House, 46 S. Middle Neck Road,
Great Neck, NY 11021, USA
Tel: (+1) 516 773 0971
Fax: (+1) 516 773 0976
E-mail: newyork@bkwsu.com

Russia, Cis And The Baltic Countries
2 Gospitalnaya Ploschad, Build. 1
Moscow - 111020, Russia
Tel: (+7) 095 263 02 47
Fax: (+7) 095 261 32 24
E-mail: bkwsu@mail.ru

http://www.bkwsu.org

Brahma Kumaris Publications
www.bkpublications.com
enquiries@bkpublications.com